BOUDICA

the British Revolt against Rome AD 60

GRAHAM WEBSTER

Routledge
Taylor & Francis Group

LONDON AND NEW YORK

First published 1978 by B.T. Batsford Ltd
Revised edition 1993

Reprinted 1999, 2003 by Routledge
11 New Fetter Lane, London EC4P 4EE

Routledge is an imprint of the Taylor & Francis Group

Typeset in Garamond
Printed and bound in Great Britain by TJ International Ltd, Padstow, Cornwall

British Library Cataloguing in Publication Data
A catalogue record for this book is available from the British Library

Library of Congress Cataloging in Publication Data
A catalogue record for this book is available from the Library of Congress

ISBN 0–415–22606–6

Contents

The Plates

Maps and Diagrams

Acknowledgements

The Author and publisher wish to thank the following for permission to
reproduce the photographs appearing in this book: The Trustees of the
British Museum, 5, 6, 18, 19, 23, 24. Cambridge University Committee for
Aerial Photography, 7. City of Cardiff, 1. City of Coventry Museum,
10, 11, 12. Colchester Castle Museum, 15, 16. Colchester Excavation
Committee, 13, 14. Norfolk Archaeological Unit, 8, 9. Society of Antiquaries of London, 2, 20, 21, 22. Verulamium Museum, 17.

Preface

My first study of this episode (*The Rebellion of Boudicca*) was written jointly with my colleague Professor Donald Dudley and published by Routledge in 1965. Since then there has been an enormous increase in archaeological knowledge from major excavations in the cities of London, Verulamium and Colchester, as well as the important work at The Lunt, near Coventry. Aerial reconnaissance has also added greatly to the number of Roman military sites and this has been followed by further investigations. As a result of all this there has been a reassessment of the Roman military operations and movements in the mid-first century. I have, therefore, felt that it was an opportune moment to present a new study, although no doubt there will be many further discoveries which will add to the story. It grieves me that my old friend Donald Dudley is no longer with us to add his eloquent and esoteric touches.

Archaeological work is a continuing process and to present the reader with the most up-to-date information and with the implications to be drawn from it, one is dependent on the help of many workers in the field. I have been very fortunate in the generosity of excavators, field workers, museum directors and flyers who have shared their new knowledge so freely with me, some of it as yet unpublished. I am especially indebted to Brian Hobley, Chief Urban Officer of the City of London, for his advice on The Lunt and information about the recent London excavations; to Margaret Rylatt his successor at Coventry, as Field Archaeologist, for further help with The Lunt and providing illustrations; to David Clarke, curator of the Colchester and Essex Museums, for help with illustrations; to Philip Crummy of the Colchester Archaeological Unit, for his helpful information about his excavations and permission to use some of his photographs; to Clive Partridge of the Hertford Archaeological Trust, for information about his discoveries at Skeleton Green, as yet unpublished; to Geoff Dannell for discussions on early imported Roman wares; to Dr John Mann for drawing my attention to an inscription and for information on an historical aspect; to Derek Edwards of the Norfolk Archaeological Trust, for the results of his aerial reconnaissance and permission to use some of his photographs and plans; to Stanley West of the Suffolk Archaeological Unit, for information about the recent work in Suffolk; to David Neal of the Department of the Environment, for information about the Gorhambury excavation; to the Society of Antiquaries of London for permission to reproduce several illustrations from their publications; to Professor J. K. S. St Joseph for supplying me with some of his superb air photographs, and to the Cambridge Committee of Aerial Photographs for permission to reproduce them; and Keith Scott for information about his discoveries at Mancetter; to Barry Eccleston for his excellent illustrations, and all friends and colleagues who have borne my questions and discussions with great patience. To Diana I owe much for her encouragement and for smoothing the text into readable English and excising the purple excesses. Mistakes of various kinds are inevitable, and I would be grateful to be told of them, just in case there is another edition.

Preface to the revised edition

The 'wronged queen' has continued to suffer in the hands of writers, few of whom have an understanding of the historical background and prefer fantasy to reality. A notable exception has been the experienced historian, Antonia Fraser, whose highly readable *Boadicea's Chariot*, 1988, follows the sequence of events established in the first edition and which is fully acknowledged. The most important new archaeological evidence comes from the publication of the excavation of a most remarkable native religious enclosure near Thetford, by the late Tony Gregory. [1] There is also an account of a large collection of finds made by years of field working by Robin Brown at Woodcock Hill near Saham Toney. This is the site of an early Roman fort and settlement on the Peddars Way, south-east of Swaffham, Norfolk.[2] Another fort has been found at Great Chesterford, Essex.[3] This appears to be an unusual size, *c.*35-37 acres, probably for a mixed force. It was possibly associated with the aftermath, of the rebellion, when 7000 troops were sent from Germany to bring units up to strength after their heavy losses.

A claim has been made and countered for the site of the last battle to have been fought near London.[4] The continuing finds of Icenian coins when they are fully analysed will add to a greater understanding of this aspect of native life and economy.

1 'Excavations in Thetford, Fison Way, 1980-1982' No. 1, *East Anglian Archaeology* Report, No. 53, 1992
2 *Brit.* 17 (1986), pp. 1-58
3 *Brit.* 3 (1972), pp. 290-3
4 *The London Archaeologist.* 4 (1984), pp. 411-13

ICENI	ATREBATES	CATUVELLAVNI	TRINOVANTES	E. KENT	OVERSEAS	DATE
						BC
					Gauls migrating in advance of Caesar in Gaul	c. 55
		CASSIVELLAVNVS	IMANVENTIVS MANDVBRACIVS		Caesar's expeditions to Britain	55–54
	COMMIVS				Commius flees from Gaul	c. 50
ANTEIOS		TASCIOVANVS	ADDEDOMAROS	DVBNOVELLAVNVS	Augustus in Gaul preparing for a British invasion	c. 30
						27
AESV [... SAEMV [...	TINCOMMIVS (c. 20)	ANDOCO [....	CVNOBELINVS		Revolt in Pannonia and Dalmatia Tincommius and Dubovellaunus suppliants in Rome (before AD 7)	AD c. 10
	EPPILLVS					1
	VERICA					6
					Disaster of Varus in Germany	9
					Death of Augustus	14
		Death of Cunobelinus c. AD 40 TOGODVMNVS			Reign of Tiberius	14–37
					Reign of Gaius (Caligula)	37–41
				ADMINIVS	Adminius flees to Gaius	39–40
	CARATACVS			CARATACVS	Reign of Claudius Verica a suppliant in Rome	41–54
PRASVTAGVS	REGNI: COGIDVBNVS					c. 41
					Roman Invasion	43

British tribes and rulers 55 BC–AD 43

Introduction

The Queen, who is known to most as Boadicea, has a place of her own in the ill-assorted pageant of folk heroes and heroines which passes in the popular mind for the history of Britain. Yet she was unknown to the medieval historians like Geoffrey of Monmouth, since they had no knowledge of the works of the Roman historian Tacitus. So the legendary figures of Bladud, King Lucius and Old King Cole held the field until the early sixteenth century. By then the manuscripts of Tacitus had been found by Boccacio in the neglected library of Monte Cassino and published in Italy. With so much new and authentic information about the early history of Britain, Polydore Virgil was able in 1534 to demolish the fanciful legends of medieval creation and set the period on a firm foundation of fact. In spite of this there were many British 'patriots' who vigorously defended the old stories and they made some headway in attacking Polydore Virgil's serious topographic errors.[1]

But the full effect of Boudica on the popular imagination was not felt until another great queen reigned, Elizabeth I. The seal was set by the Italian soldier and courtier Petruccio Ubaldini in his book *The Lives of the Noble Ladies of the Kingdom of England and Scotland*. The muddled geography of Polydore Virgil led to Boudica becoming two separate women, Voadicia, a northern queen, and Bunduica, and to the version given by Tacitus being separated from that of the Greek historian Cassius Dio, who had taken most of his evidence from Tacitus. As an account also appeared in Holinshed's *Chronicles*, it is likely that Shakespeare may have thought about using it, as he had done with King Lear and Cymbeline; but it was left to his contemporary, Fletcher, to produce his *Bonduca* in 1610. Perhaps there was an anti-climax after the death of Elizabeth, or maybe there was another reason for his chief character being Caratach, based on Caratacus, instead of the queen.

The story appears in the accounts by seventeenth- and eighteenth-century historians, but the most important protagonist was the poet Cowper whose 'Ode' of 1780 on the story of Boadicea remained extremely popular for a long time. The same can hardly be said of the effort of Lord Tennyson, but the fault of his *Boadicea* lies not in the subject but the strange metre he chose, deliberately imitating Catullus. It is technically a *tour de force* but virtually unreadable and has sunk into the oblivion it may well deserve.

It was under a third great queen, Victoria, that interest in Boudica revived. The 1850s was the time when the British became aware of their growing wealth and vastly expanding Empire, which led not only to grandiose conceptions like the Great Exhibition, but a conscious backward look at the glories of Britain's past. These feelings linked with the dominating figure of the reigning queen inspired one of the leading sculptors, Thomas Thorncroft, who had already carried out commissions for the Royal Family. His concept was a colossal group portraying Boudica in her war chariot and a pair of rearing horses. This remarkable piece of Victorian grandeur was encouraged by Prince Albert, but the work was so prodigious that both he and the sculptor died before it could be completed, leaving only the plaster casts. It was not until 1902 that the funds and the site were available. So Boudica now confronts the Embankment with the House of Commons and Big Ben at her back, as if she was defending the very embodiment of the kind of Establishment she tried so hard to destroy. Ideas and attitudes have changed over the last century and this bronze group may now seem to us a prodigious folly in doubtful taste, and the archaeologist sneers at the chariot with the scythes on the wheels and its ponderous armoured bulk – the very antithesis of the beautiful light wicker-work vehicle we now know the British chariot to have been.

Yet there she stands today, an image imprinted in the minds of the vast majority of Britons, and may even create an emotive patriotic stir at the thought of the virago of a queen defying a great but alien power. It may seem to many mere pedantry to seek to change this popular concept based on such noble sentiments. But the truth must emerge into the light of day and be seen to be, as it surely is, even more exciting and thought-provoking than the cardboard image for all its tinsel and bold colours. This is the task we have set ourselves.

1

Sources

When Queen Victoria travelled on her exciting tour of northern Scotland in 1872, she found many roads decked with triumphal arches bearing messages in Gaelic AR BUIDHEACHAS DO'N BHUADHAICH – 'To Victoria, our gratitude'.[1] Here the Gaelic shows the connection with the distant Celtic tongue, in the word for victory – *bouda*, which in modern Welsh is *buddug*.[2] The name of the famous queen of the Iceni was actually Boudīcā, which meant precisely 'Victoria'. The word appears in similar forms on inscriptions, one of the most interesting of which was found in Bordeaux in 1921. It is an altar to the goddess Tutela Boudiga, the local deity called 'the victorious'.[3] Another example of Boudica as a personal name appears on a stone in Lusitania.[4] But this is not the version which has come down to us from the Latin historian Tacitus. First of all Tacitus himself got it wrong by giving the lady two 'c's calling her Boudicca; then someone copied a manuscript in the Middle Ages inscribed an 'a' instead of a 'u' and an 'e' instead of the second 'c' – quite easy mistakes to make. Thus the romantic Victorian poets helped to perpetrate this error which still remains with us, since most people know her as Queen Boadicea. Her actual name is Boudica, and that is what we will continue to use in this study. The name is the only link between these two great women, both enshrined in British history but separated by almost two millennia. We know much about Queen Victoria, some of it in great detail, what she ate and what she thought, although the historians still complain about the loss of important personal papers.

ANCIENT HISTORIANS

Boudica will always remain in the grey shadow of history, since all we know of her is to be found in two classical writers who may have derived most of their material from the same original source. Tacitus, the Roman senator and consul was writing his *Annals* only fifty years after the event. He had access to the Imperial archives, but above all Gnaeus Iulius Agricola was his father-in-law. Agricola became Governor of Britain in AD 78 and we know of his campaigns against the tribes of Scotland from his biography by Tacitus. However, Agricola is unique among Roman military men in serving three terms in the same province on the ascending ladder in the career of a Roman senator. His first military appointment was as a tribune, the senior of five officers and known as *tribunus laticlavius*, i.e. of the broad strip (on the *toga*) signifying his senatorial status, the other tribunes being of the equestrian order; then as legionary commander, of *Legio* XX *Valeria*, and finally as Governor. It was during his three-year appointment as a tribune that the Revolt took place. Agricola would have known about it in detail, and he may even have taken part in the main military action. Unfortunately, of the four legions in Britain at that time, we do not know which was the one in which he served, but a case could be made for IInd *Augusta*, then at Exeter. It was customary for governors on important campaigns to appoint senior officers from legions, not actually engaged, as staff officers to his command HQ. This could have applied to Agricola and may account for the IInd *Augusta* being under the command of the third officer in the chain of legionary command, the *praefectus castrorum*, at a critical moment, but more of that later. The point to be made here is that Agricola could have given Tacitus an eyewitness account of the events, as well as a shrewd political commentary. But Tacitus was too good an historian to magnify single events in a remote province out of proportion in his vast sweep of Imperial history. So his account, although of undoubted accuracy, is over-concise and we could now wish he had indulged his knowledge, even to mentioning the part played by his father-in-law. But, to the stiff, unbending Roman, it would have been improper to introduce family matters into his great political tract (for the *Annals* is a piece of propaganda, and, although on a vast canvas, has a remarkable balance and was written with consummate craft). We have to make what we can of his account, which includes only the more significant details, omitting so much of interest and importance, as we attempt to piece together the fragments of this intricate jig saw.

Cassius Dio, our other source, was a Greek historian writing at the end of the second century. His *History of Rome* has many faults, since he accepted his sources uncritically and much of his lengthy work has only survived in the form of epitomies. These are not précis but careful selections. The choice of the material was not made so much for readers of history, but to provide suitable dramatic passages for readings. Public and private readings were a feature of life in high society in classical times, and there were highly skilled professionals who could be hired for these occasions. This practice can be linked with all the deep Roman interest in rhetoric, one of the chief subjects in the school curriculum. The motivation was not a political one but the necessity for it in the law courts, one of the chief means of advancement open to those of the right social background.

Not only did it bring political rewards but great wealth to the skilled advocate, and the Roman passion for litigation seems boundless. It was not the pen which was mightier than the sword, but the golden tongue. Reading was regarded by most as a tiresome necessity, and those who indulged in it were the philosophers who were despised by the normal conservative Roman to whom tradition was a sacred element in the fabric of society. So the fashionable dinner parties included readings between the many courses, and this helps to explain the way in which the 'epitomators' made their selections.

They provided passages suitable for such occasions, and where the historical events demanded speeches, these were the high points in the performance. Great pains were taken in the arrangement and wording of these pieces of rhetoric put into the mouths of the chief protagonists. Very often the occasion was a battle before which the commanders addressed their forces. It would have been impossible in most circumstances for these men to have delivered the bombastic pieces of rhetoric found in the histories. Orders of the day, before an engagement, had to be curt and to the point. Tacitus appreciated this and apart from Caesar, one of the few such speeches that he records is the one attributed to Suetonius Paullinius before the decisive battle against Boudica.

> Ignore the din made by these barbarians and their empty threats, there are more women than men in their ranks. They are not soldiers, nor are they properly equipped, we have beaten them before and when they see our weapons and valour they'll crack – what glory awaits you, our small fame will win the renown of the whole army, stick together, throw the javelins, strike forward with your shield bosses, finish them off with your swords, forget about booty, go in and win and you'll have the lot.

This is blunt soldier talk probably heard by Agricola who passed it on to Tacitus. Quite different is the account by Dio, which includes three speeches delivered to different bodies of troops. They are neat pieces of rhetoric, not the sensible practical words which have a touch of reality. Apart from these two accounts, the whole event is treated in a single sentence by Suetonius Tranquillus in his *Biographies of the Twelve Caesars*. There is also an important comment attributed to Nero – the idea of withdrawing his forces from Britain. Unfortunately, this is not placed in any context and will have to be considered in the more detailed discussion below.

If one had only the historical account, one could speculate endlessly on the campaigns and this is precisely what the antiquaries of the past did and continue to do. The siting of the last great battle has created in elderly gentlemen that furious obstinacy which only comes from the certain feeling of being absolutely right. With much waving of umbrellas and walking sticks, have come some strange ideas, the oddest perhaps that the battle was fought under platform 10 at King's Cross Station.[6]

B

THE CONTRIBUTION OF ARCHAEOLOGY

The growth of knowledge and the development of archaeology as a more precise study enable us now to take a more objective and sober view. The new evidence comes from three main sources. There is the find made casually by the plough or in cutting a drainage trench, which, when identified by a discerning eye, might give a hint of something worth examining on the ground. If this kind of discovery is fully recorded and placed in a local museum, identification and study can follow and with that its possible significance. We know much more than we did some years ago about the kind of military equipment used by different units of the Roman army, and the finding of even small fragments which could be recognised might well lead towards the discovery of a fort. These small and often heavily corroded pieces of metal have belonged to a legionary or an auxiliary or infantry or cavalry, or perhaps a specialist unit. Many fragments exist already in our museums which are wonderful storehouses of knowledge, often untapped, since so many of these collections have never been fully studied or published. It is here that one might begin a study of the distribution of specific types of archaeological artefacts. I well remember my excitement on a casual visit to the Scunthorpe Museum, noticing on display a tiny scrap of bronze from Owmby Cliffe, a well-known Roman site half-way on the road north from Lincoln to the Humber. It had a peculiar shape which made it instantly identifiable to me as a hinge of Roman infantry armour and could indicate a military presence at this place. Some finds are published, many in old reports, where they may be both badly drawn and wrongly described. It was a group of bronzes, rather poorly illustrated in an annual report of the Thoroton Society,[7] that first drew my attention to the possibility of an early fort at Broxstow near Nottingham. But, alas, by that time most of the site was covered by a council housing estate.

While there is still much to be discovered in museums and old reports in the journals of national and county archaeological societies, the main source of new information now comes from excavations. It is difficult for the layman to appreciate the great change which has taken place in British archaeological attitudes and practice over the last few decades, since the reporting of such matters in the media is still ridden with antiquated and romantic ideas, more often linked with treasure hunting. During the last war the Government recognised the need to examine sites being destroyed by the building of airfields, army camps and new factories, and a small amount of money was put aside for this. It kept several archaeologists busy for some years, the chief among them was that superb excavator Professor W.F. Grimes, who was later to become Director of the Institute of Archaeology at the University of London. With his high standard of excavation and publication,[8] he could claim to be the father of modern rescue archaeology. The department responsible for this rescue work was the Ancient Monuments Division of what was at that time the Office of Works, the chief responsibility of which was the maintenance of royal castles and the implementation of the ancient monuments acts.

With hindsight it could be argued that this was not an appropriate department to develop a policy of large-scale rescue excavations and, at first, its inspectors accepted this ever-widening responsibility with some reluctance. It was some time before specialist staff were appointed, much of the work being placed in the hands of outside directors who were appointed as the need arose. The absence of a permanent team, and the total lack of continuity or an effective publication policy, created a serious situation which brought a pressure group called 'Rescue' into being.[9] The result has been a large increase in the rescue budget, the appointment of full-time staff and the establishment of rescue excavation on a more satisfactory basis thoughout the country.

Even under the difficult and often frustrating conditions of the last few years, rescue archaeology has developed at an amazing pace and in terms of manpower and production has far surpassed the old-fashioned small-scale rescue excavations, made inadequate by the pitifully meagre resources then available. These earlier efforts are now seen as a very limited kind of exercise, useful only in defining the area of a site or testing its potentialities. Excavation has become, quite suddenly, a large-scale highly organised operation, requiring large sums of money, involving the stripping and careful examination of large areas at a time. It is a highly professional job, employing specialist surveyors, technicians and conservation staff, with elaborate recording systems often designed for computer analysis and data retrieval.

The scientific aspects alone have become of great importance with the growth of environmental archaeology, which deals with the reconstruction of the landscapes and ecologies of the past through a study of buried soils, plant and insect remains, animal bones and so on. The result of all this work has been a vastly accelerating rate of discovery, bringing with it a torrent of new information about our past. Much of this has challenged some of the basic concepts of the periods we thought safe from any major reconsideration. It will, however, be some years before the new evidence can be fully assimilated and the results appear in popular accounts for the general public.

In the historical events with which we are here concerned, the basic chronological framework laid down by the ancient historians, Tacitus and Cassius Dio, can hardly be challenged. What rescue archaeology has done is to add greatly to the disposition and movement of Roman forces. This gives a greater clarity to the whole and adds that essential dimension of reality.

Most of our historic towns and cities are being ruthlessly 'developed' to provide future generations with massive blocks of unlovely concrete and glass structures which look the same the world over. The loss in the style and variation of local material and architecture which made our old towns so interesting and attractive is sad, but the people of the future, looking at pictures of those forgotten street scenes, will only think how small and inconvenient they must have been. This feeling of the past is more acute with those of us who knew and loved the atmosphere of these ancient lanes and buildings. The work of destruction has been rapid and widespread, and there has been little time or money for the slow process of excavations necessary in those places where the early remains are so deep and complicated. Nevertheless, a little has been salvaged and out of this comes evidence bearing on the events of AD 60. Our ancient authors tell us that three Roman cities were destroyed – at London, Colchester and St Albans, known as Londinium, Camulodunum and Verulamium. Thick destruction layers, covering burnt timber buildings, have been found in all three places.

Excavation policy is now almost entirely dictated by the pressures of development, and much of the information retrieved is often sporadic and unconnected, since there is money only for work on the sites where new buildings are planned and rarely on sites which one would choose for gaining the maximum amount of information. To a certain extent this is fortunate since new knowledge can turn up in the most unexpected places, confounding ideas which can easily conform to patterns some archaeologists may be reluctant to change. It makes those who are humble enough realise just how little is really known. Occasionally, even now some excavations are carried out as research projects unimpeded by development which is so limiting in time and space. It so happens that one of the most important pieces of research work has been on a military site established as a result of the Revolt. The work at The Lunt at Baginton, near Coventry, was directed by Brian Hobley on behalf of Coventry Corporation where he was then Field Officer. The results are so important and fascinating that a separate section has been devoted to them.

AERIAL RECONNAISSANCE

The third of our major sources of information comes from aerial reconnaissance. A position a thousand feet or so above the earth gives a wonderful sense of landscape and prompts questions about the natural and human activities which have created such a diverse pattern. Above all, it is an excellent place from which to appraise the military factors, provided one fully understands the limitations of movement and fire power at each period. Many a retired army officer has applied himself to the campaigns of the Roman army without a full appreciation of the tactics and logistics involved. The appearance of the landscape too has drastically changed through the ages, especially that of the rivers which had not in those times been made captive between their banks, but were free to spread and move about within their wide valley bottoms. This is why crossing places were so important and this was the reason for the ancient trackways, which led to the places where there was firm ground on both sides of the river, rather than attempting to cross a mile or more of marsh and mud. It is only with recent years that ecologists have begun to study the details of the ancient landscapes from the scraps of evidence which survive as buried soils and old river courses. Man's taming of the natural landscape has been a lengthy process, varying from time to time and including periods of recession, during which the woods and rivers have spread unchecked. It may be long before maps can be prepared showing the local geography at all stages of this fascinating progress and decline in human affairs.

The view from the air in lowland Britain is that of a man-made landscape, most of it no more than 200–300 years old. But there are traces to be seen of earlier features, indicating settlement and field patterns. These belong usually to the Middle Ages when plagues and ruthless farm management, mainly by the large monasteries, swept away whole villages. These have often remained fossilised in the landscape as bumps and hollows which resolve themselves into house platforms and hollowed trackways. This kind of site shows up very well from the air when the sun is low in the sky, casting long shadows which exaggerate the smallest changes in the ground surface.[10]

It is rare for any surface remains of such a remote period as the first century to survive in the lowland zone, which has been continuously ploughed for almost 2,000 years. But Roman forts do occasionally stand up as rectangular platforms originally created by the spread of material after demolition, especially from the rampart. This could have raised the site of the fort one or two feet above the surrounding area, an effect that is accentuated by the sinkage in the surrounding ditches. There is a fort along Watling Street at Pennocrucium, where such a platform is visible but is brought out sharply from the air, since the raised area became a small medieval field with a distinctive plough pattern.

Most of the earlier sites show up by a different process known as cropmarks. This is the pattern of differential colours of a crop at certain times of the year, especially during ripening. If, as is often the case, the fort was built on a dry, well-drained subsoil, such as sand or gravel, the moisture in the subsoil drains away quickly and, at a time of drought, the growing crops may be deficient in the water that is so necessary to bring the nutrients from the soil to the head of the plant. When this happens the crop tends to ripen more rapidly than usual. In the case of a ditch cut well into the subsoil and later filled in and levelled, the material in the ditch will not be so clean and sandy as the natural strata into which it has been cut, but will contain pieces of clay, plant remains and debris from the demolition of the fort. Thus the ditch will retain enough moisture to help the plants growing

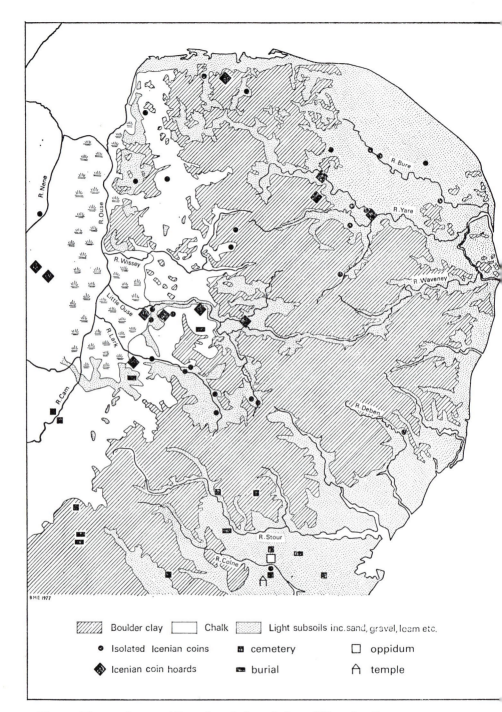

R. Nene

R. Ouse

R. Wissey

Little Ouse

R. Lark

R. Cam

R. Bure

R. Yare

R. Waveney

R. Deben

R. Stour

R. Colne

BME 1977

	Boulder clay		Chalk		Light subsoils inc.sand, gravel, loam etc.

⦿ Isolated Icenian coins   ▪ cemetery   ☐ oppidum

◆ Icenian coin hoards   ▬ burial   ⌂ temple

Fig. 1   The geology and Iron Age finds and sites of East Anglia

over it to have a slower rate of growth than those ripening in drier conditions. The effect of this natural process can be quite startling; at a critical time, which may be only a day or so, the plants over the ditch remain a lush green, while those in the rest of the field have turned yellow. The flyer sees below the green lines and, if these are over the fort ditches, they conform to the normal plan of a rectangle with beautifully rounded corners, and so are instantly identifiable.

One must appreciate, however, that it is not as simple as this. Activities which have caused intrusions in the subsoil can be very varied and happen at any time. Farmers may dig large holes to bury cattle stricken by some dreaded plague, or, more likely, lay lines or drains all over the fields, grub up hedges and fill in ditches. These and many other works of improvement or disposal, create crop-marks as well as the basic geological differences already present in the subsoil. Then too, the time of the year is critical, as well as a close study of the weather and the stage of crop growth, which may differ from field to field. So aerial reconnaissance has become not only expensive but a highly professional task, and the work of studying and interpreting the photographs even more so.

There is no doubt, however, that results from this source on the study of the Roman army in Britain have been very considerable. Hundreds of sites have been added to our list, far more than could have been found on the ground by fieldwork and excavation, even if adequate resources had been available. In most cases a study of the photographs and a quick view of the sites at ground level are all we can accomplish at present. This means that it is impossible to date the sites unless they show a feature in defence construction peculiar to a certain period, nor can one have any appreciation of the arrangement of the buildings inside, or of the kind of soldiers and units occupying them. This, as will be seen, has produced problems which may be subject to differing interpretations, and a good example is the series of forts of about 20–30 acres. Since this is about half that required for a legion, they have been called vexillation fortresses, implying that it was occupied by a mixed force or that legions were split in two. But only large scale detailed excavation will provide the solution, but not so easily identify the type of unit.

It will be evident from this chapter that, although there may have been great advances in knowledge over the last two or three decades, we are still groping around in a field of bewildering complexity and difficulty. All we can now do is to lay down a few guidelines and consider what is at present known, and what we can deduce from this knowledge, about the catastrophic events of AD 60.

2

The Opposing Forces
and the State of Britain 54 BC

Any attempt to follow the campaigns and battles and to understand Roman army tactics and general strategy would be fraught with difficulties without a basic understanding of the Imperial army of this period.[1] As an organisation it was never allowed to become a rigid structure incapable of change and adopting new ideas – a serious fault often found in most other armies. The reason for this is simply that Rome was hardly ever at peace: somewhere along the great stretch of frontiers there were hostile elements to be watched and engaged. In some areas the *pax Romana* may have extended over several generations, but such was the diversity of the enemy that tacticians were always concerned with methods of dealing with new threats. The army was in a constant state of change – not always for the best. On occasions a decline set in and softness and laxity became endemic, so that strong leaders were forced to reforge the rusty weapons, bring in new blood and develop fresh ideas.

In the middle of the first century, the army was still pursuing a policy of aggression and attack. The idea of a finite frontier with a highly organised defensive hinterland was yet in the future. It was a confident body preferring always to engage in open warfare, rather than to take up strong positions of defence. The training and discipline, the superb equipment, high morale and innate sense of destiny made it superior to any Celtic force, even with ten times the number of men. It is essentially the difference between the professional and the amateur. The Britons were no mean fighters, as they had already demonstrated, but they were cast in the heroic mould, not far removed from Homer's warriors of ancient Troy. To the Celts, fighting was a necessary ingredient of manhood and initiation into it was often decided by individual combat. Tribal disputes were sometimes decided by two chosen warriors like Hector and Achilles, who fought it out while both armies watched, like the vociferous and excitable football supporters of today. Where the two armies differed so much, is that, once the battle was engaged, the Britons were committed to a predetermined course of action. The Romans, on the other hand, were trained to change their tactics by disengaging units, moving them about, altering the balance of strength in the front line and developing intricate manoeuvres, feinting here, pressing there or enveloping a flank. They had tactical drill books and a highly organised signalling system. The troops were disciplined and trained to obey instantly and move into new positions. Thus the Roman officers could control the course of a battle; they were never allowed to become a set-piece which could only develop into a slogging match. This is why time and time again the Romans engaged a barbarian horde many times their number and carved it into separated parts, which they could annihilate with skilled precision.

But the Britons had their successes too, not however by attempting open pitched battles, for they soon discovered they had an edge on the Romans when it came to guerilla tactics on their own terrain. In thick woodlands, the Romans were deprived of the use of their cavalry to search out the enemy and rout small groups. In their own forests and marshes, which the Britons knew so well, they could take the Romans by surprise, create havoc and casualties, then melt away and vanish as suddenly as they had appeared. When they pursued these tactics, the Britons were successful. In the difficult country west of the Severn, they frustrated Roman attempts at control and caused such heavy losses that in AD 54 the Roman government under Nero thought seriously of giving up Britain altogether. Had the Britons persisted with these tactics, they might have achieved their aim of forcing Rome to withdraw from the Province. They kept hoping, however, that sheer weight of numbers could cower and crush the small Roman forces – only to fail catastrophically.

Before considering strategy and tactics in detail, it is necessary to give a brief review of the organisation of the army. At this period the main fighting strength rested with the legions. Originally it was a citizen army and one still had to be a Roman citizen to join, with the officer grades largely recruited from Italy. But by the middle of the first century it had become the practice to recruit tough barbarians from the frontier areas to fill the ranks, enrolling them as citizens when they took the oath, even though they could hardly speak a word of Latin. All Roman units were organised on a *milliary* or *quingenary* basis, i.e. 1,000 or 500 strong, although the actual number had become established at a somewhat lower figure.

Thus, one has to think of the legion as ten cohorts, nine of which were *quingeni* and one *milliarius*, which was the first cohort of hand-picked, seasoned men, the core of the legion. Each of the nine 'normal' cohorts consisted of six 'centuries' of 80 men, led by a centurion, but the first had five double centuries commanded by centurions of senior rank. The chief centurion was the *primus pilus*, a much coveted position, which raised the holder automatically into equestrian status after a year in this position; thereafter lucrative positions were open to him in the higher ranks of the army and in the Imperial civil service. A simplified view of the internal arrangements of the legion would truly be misleading as it was extremely complicated and is only partially understood.[2] The legionaries normally retired after fifteen years' service, but this was a rather irregular procedure at this time. Centurions never retired but went on in service until they died – except the *primipilares* who went on to higher office.

The senior officers were the commander (*legatus legionis*) and the six tribunes, five of equestrian rank and a senator designate, acting mainly in legal and administrative roles. It is difficult for us to understand a system in which the military and civil functions are so interlocked. It is as if our politicians and company directors had to spend part of their careers as senior army officers (as indeed some successfully did in wartime). Normal Roman practice was for members of the senatorial order to take command, not only in the army, but also as provincial governors. Those of the equestrian order, i.e. the knightly class, had similar careers, but in lower grades. If one is born into such a well-established social order the system can operate reasonably well. Obviously individuals vary greatly in their abilities and capacities. Thus, those who failed vanished into obscurity and those who grew in office were given greater responsibility according to their particular talents. Provincial governors and legionary commanders were chosen with care. When a province faced serious threats from attack or revolt, an experienced general with a well-proven record was sent to deal with it. If, however, a province was in financial difficulties or tribes needed pacification and reorganisation a very different person was chosen. Occasionally mistakes were made. One of the worst was when Augustus sent Varus to Germany to integrate the legal system into the Roman pattern. He had not imagined that the governor was to be faced with such a serious frontier situation, which led him into a trap with the loss of three legions. Augustus was deeply affected by this tragedy since the mistake had clearly been his alone.

The legions bore the brunt of the fighting, especially in a set-piece engagement and the men were well equipped for this tough hand-to-hand warfare. They all wore body armour arranged in horizontal strips which were strong and flexible, allowing full arm movement and it was strengthened on the shoulders with additional curved strips.[3] They had well-designed helmets which also covered the neck and cheeks. They could take sword blows aimed from above as well as from the front and back, but their legs were unprotected, since any weight here would have prevented rapid movement and tired them on long marches. But the chief protection came from the large shield, curved to fit the whole of the left side of the body from chin to knee. The edges were bound in metal but the shield itself was made of thin sheets of wood glued together with cross grain, somewhat like our own plywood; the front was covered with red leather and decorated with bronze mounts in the form of stylised thunderbolts and flashes of lightning, the emblems of Jupiter, the senior Roman deity. Every man had two javelins, each seven feet long, with a wooden shaft and iron shank and hardened tip. These were normally thrown in two volleys at the advancing enemy, and were designed to penetrate the enemy shields, so that in the heat of the moment they were cast aside.

It was only at this point that the legionaries drew their short swords, carried high up on the right-hand side for ease of withdrawal and so as to not impede the shield side. They closed formation into a line of tight wedges, brought their shields close into their bodies, then suddenly and violently projected themselves into the enemy mass, pushing forward with the heavy metal shield boss and using the sword like a bayonet, thrusting and turning into the soft parts of the bodies. With this rapid forward thrust and by their very weight, they carved their way through the enemy ranks, driving them back against one another, packing the Celtic warriors so tightly together that they could not use their long swords. For the legionaries did not need space to continue their instant butchery, but pushed forward eagerly trampling over the falling bodies with their heavy hob-nail boots. These brutal, but effective tactics go a long way to explain the success of the legions against greater numbers.

The Roman conception of warfare was simple and logical. This was the total destruction of the enemy on the field of battle. But it could not be achieved by the legionaries alone. As soon as the tide of battle turned, the enemy would run and attempt to escape. To prevent this, cavalry units were waiting on each wing for this moment. When it came, they charged forward with lances and sword, cutting down those in flight from behind, or rounding them into the middle like frightened cattle to await the grim legionaries now advancing with speed and menace. Those who threw down their arms and cried for mercy rarely got it if there had been serious Roman casualties to be avenged. However, the victorious soldiers might now think of booty and begin to select prisoners from the younger and more healthy specimens cowering before them : the thought of a good price in the slave market could stay the sword arm. Now that their work was done, their attention also could turn to the gold and silver torques and bracelets worn by the Celtic chieftains.

THE BRITONS[4]

What had the Britons to offer against such highly organised, ruthless professionalism? Bravery was there in plenty and, for many the basic concept that they were fighting for their freedom against foreign domination. To this must be added a religious element, which, as we shall see, also became an important political factor. The Druidic hierarchy was recruited from the tribal aristocracy, who were concerned with the survival of a social order and the maintenance of authority. But the great mass of feudal levies was inspired only with the feeling of loyalty to their chiefs and their tribe, and just how much this counted in a tight situation could depend on the personality of their leader.

The degree of social integration and tribal response to authority can be judged from the hill-forts. Some are very large and the defences massive enough to have needed considerable well-organised manpower for their construction. This implies that the tribal chiefs could expect unquestioned obedience in heavy manual tasks, although there was also the element of tribal and self protection. Warfare was part of the Celtic way of life, involving from early times the initiation of the young males into manhood. Fighting, regarded as a kind of sport, was given many opportunities in the constant cattle raiding and border forays. Warfare on a tribal footing was only necessary when territory had to be defended against an aggressive policy of expansion by an ambitious neighbour; levies had then to be mobilised and concentrated, but there was a limit to the time during which their enthusiasm and loyalty could be held; the men would soon want to return to their farms and families, especially if there were long periods of waiting. This is obvious from Caesar's account of his activities in Britain: Cassivellaunus, the commander-in-chief, could only harass Caesar's advance beyond the Thames with his charioteers, since the levies had melted away, after a serious set-back south of the river (V. 17).

The main difference between the opposing forces was between amateurs and professionals, but the situation was not quite as clear-cut as this. The chiefs could rely on a hand-picked bodyguard of young retainers who, trained in hand-to-hand fighting, could be effective against small groups of Romans, but they could not face the full weight of a legion with auxiliary support. The mass of British levies lacked organisation, discipline and equipment. The best body protection a man could acquire was a leather jerkin, heavily greased to turn a swordblade, with toughened strips or patches to the shoulders and other vulnerable parts. But the more one wore, the more difficult it was to use one's weapons effectively. This is why many Britons preferred to fight naked, relying on the magic of the woad-painted symbols on their bodies, which also gave them a frightening appearance (Caesar, V. 14). There was no lack of skill among the Celtic blacksmiths and bronze workers, but, as in the Middle Ages, they produced fine individual pieces for the chiefs and their young warrior retinue. The idea of mass-producing of weapons and armour for the levies never arose: they were lucky to have a reliable sword. Yet, if we are to believe Caesar, Cassivellaunus could rely on 4,000 charioteers and the swordsmen they carried. This suggests that the chiefs of the south-east had made contributions from their personal forces.

The chariot,[5] the most interesting aspect of British warfare, had become outmoded everywhere else but in these islands and the sandy wastes of the Near East. (It is strange that through the ages Britain has clung to out-of-date military concepts – an inherent conservatism associated no doubt with her insularity.) Caesar had a keen eye for the unusual, especially in warfare, and must by now have realised his remarkable gifts as a commander. He knew his readers would appreciate a piece of odd drollery to leaven the unending account of his victories against savage and unrelenting foes in such enormous numbers. So he gives a detailed description of the British chariot in action:

> The way they fight from chariots is thus: first they drive in all directions throwing their spears to inspire terror which added to the noise of the wheels throws the enemy ranks into confusion. When they have penetrated the cavalry units they leap from their chariots and fight on foot, while the charioteers gradually withdraw from the fray and so place the chariots, that, should the fighters become hard-pressed by the numbers of the enemy, they can easily slip away to their own lines. Thus they have the mobility of cavalry with the stability of the infantry, and by daily exercises and use, that they become so proficient that they drive their horses down the steepest slopes under complete control, stop and turn quickly run along the pole, stand on the yoke and quickly back to the chariot.

The kind of vehicles to carry out these difficult manoeuvres must have had special qualities such as lightness for speed and quick turning, yet toughness to stand up to the rough going and heavy treatment. These obvious and necessary qualities did not prevent Victorian and even later artists depicting something quite different. There is a fine example in the great memorial to Boudica mentioned in the Introduction. This chariot, a remarkable piece of romantic fiction, has a heavy metal body with solid wheels, unlikely to move far in muddy ground, even drawn by such large splendid and spirited horses. But the aspect which has seized popular fancy more than anything, is the pair of curved, vicious looking, knives fixed to the axles. This delightfully horrific detail will doubtless remain fixed in the nation's mind as the image of the Britons and Boudica in particular, like Alfred's cakes and Bruce's spider. Such is the rich tapestry of our national history, and it almost seems sacriligious to attempt to challenge it. But the archaeologists are persistent ferrets sniffing out the truth.

The people in Britain were in those days almost as mixed as they are now. British stock is an amalgam of folk moving intermittently westwards and northwards from the great land mass of Europe and settling in Britain because they had reached the edge of the known world. It could be argued that the sea crossing in ancient times was so dangerous for their flimsy craft, that those who reached these shores were only the bravest and most determined of their kind, and thus, some of our national characteristics may be due to this form of selection. As the country near the southern and eastern coasts became fully occupied the newcomers had to fight for a foothold, and if successful, enslave or push out the settlers who were already there. This led to a gradual drift of the weaker folk towards the north and west. By the time of the Roman conquest, the more recent migrants, who had established themselves in the south-east, were the most civilised, having close connections with their Gallic kinsfolk. Most of those who occupied the mountain areas to the west and north had been forced to settle there under the pressures of land hunger from the south. However, not all the migrants originated from Gaul or the Low Countries. Those who started from the Iberian peninsula would make a land fall on the western sea coast and, if they did not favour the rather inhospitable coast of Cornwall, could venture west and drift into the safer waters of the Bristol Channel.

By the first century Britain was well populated and the large number of defended sites, mainly on hill tops, shows the need to protect territory from intruders and raiders. The very scale and complexity of some of these defences demonstrated not only their engineering skills, but also their ability to organise people to carry out massive earth-shifting and ditch-digging. Just how these tribes were governed and related to each other is obscure, but a study of the distribution pattern of their coins gives some indication of the Gallic migrations to Britain, of their main areas of settlement and of the subsequent conflicts between them and the peoples who had established themselves after earlier migrations.

The evidence of Gallic and British coins
The idea of coinage and its usefulness in trade came to the west from the Graeco-Roman world. The first coins minted by the Celts in Gaul were copies, the most famous and widespread of which was an issue of Philip II of Macedon with the head of Apollo on one side and a two-horse chariot on the other, symbolising the daily journey of the sun across the sky. In the repeated copying of this coin, the original designs were soon lost, and in the British examples the head of the god degenerated into the diagonal lines of blobs and crescents which were all that remained of the laurel wreath; while the chariot, horse and driver became a few bent lines derived from the horses' legs and a detached wheel or so from the chariot.

Caesar gives us the useful information that there had been peoples from Gaul invading Britain and settling here, and these Gauls had preserved ties of kinship with those who remained behind, up to the time of the Gallic conquest. Caesar states that one in particular, the great King Diviciacus of the Suessiones, claimed to have ruled over parts of Britain, as well as Gaul. It was in Caesar's interest to propagate the belief that the tribes of Britain and Gaul had close political ties, and that the Britons were capable of supporting the Gauls against him. He could use this as the justification for his intervention in Britain at a time when his own political future seemed to be at stake and he was anxious to extend his sphere of influence. Although this may create a doubt over the statements he made concerning his own immediate problem, there is no reason to reject the historical background. There is sound archaeological evidence in the form of coins, pottery and burial rites to suggest a series of invasions starting about 50 BC. The coins give us a clearer picture, and this is due entirely to the painstaking work of Derek Allen over many years in his basic study of the various types of Celtic coins and his arrangement of them into a chronological series.[6]

The earliest coin types found in Britain are the Gallo-Belgic A and B, which were minted and used in Gaul between *c.* 150 and 50 BC. The British distribution of these types is centred on the Thames Estuary, and it is interesting that all these coins have been struck from dies which have been deliberately defaced, as if, it has been suggested, they belonged to migrants who were thus symbolically cutting themselves off from their homelands. This may seem a fanciful idea, but it is difficult to think of a better explanation. The distribution pattern, together with the numbers and concentrations of the coins, strongly indicates settlement, rather than trade. Warwick Rodwell, in an important study,[7] has attempted to isolate three main areas of primary Gallic settlement: (1) on the Medway Estuary with Rochester at the centre; (2) a small area on the tip of north-east Kent; and the Colne peninsula centred on (3) Camulodunum. This does not necessarily mean that large groups of people were on the move, since the same effect could have been achieved by bands of warrior aristocrats asserting their authority over native populations. This suggestion may be corroborated by the absence of archaeological evidence, other than coins; no one has yet been able to point to a new kind of pottery to be associated with the coins, so the newcomers must have used the wares made here. This idea has been supported by the distribution of a coarse ware, isolated by Ann Birchall[8] and published by Warwick Rodwell (his fig. 14). This ware appears in areas of the possible early Gallo-Belgic settlements.

The tribal boundaries shown on the map of Roman-Britain are extremely vague, since there is so little precise information. It would appear, however, that the area ascribed to the Catuvellauni is very considerable. The only certain boundary would have been the River Thames on the south, to the east were the Trinovantes, presumably east of the River Lea. To the north-east were the Iceni and to the north the Corieltauvi (previously mistakenly known as the Coritani) but in neither case are there any physical features on which to base boundaries. One can also assume that the Catuvellauni were formed out of a group of smaller tribes. In the list of the five British allies given by Caesar only the Cenimagni (Iceni) is known. There are names on coins such as Sego, Riconi, Dias, Rues and Andoc but it is not possible to know which are tribal names or those of rulers. Only with Sego on a coin of Tasciovanus could one suggest a short form of Segontiaci in Caesar's list, but there is as yet no survival known of the other three, i.e. Ancalites, Bibroci and Cassi.

The next 'wave' of coins reaching Britain is a very important one, but difficult to understand. This is the Gallo-Belgic C, which dated to *c.*, 60 BC, is linked with Diviciacus.[1] It has been argued that as only just over twenty coins of this type have been found in Britain, they do not represent a new wave of settlement, but an extension of power by the high king of the Suessiones. One of the most puzzling and interesting aspects of Gallo-Belgic C is that it was this type of coin which was first copied by the Britons. But this did not happen, as one might expect, in those areas in contact with these coins, but in Hampshire and Wiltshire, the territory of the Durotriges; yet there are only two examples of the Gallic issues known in this area, and both on the coast. A possible explanation could be that Diviciacus was exerting diplomatic pressure in these areas in an effort to seek alliances, and one of the ways in which this could be achieved was by helping the British kings to produce their own coins. These new British issues may have had little economic impact, but the prestige value could have been considerable. This is demonstrated by the rapidity with which it spread, for there are no less than eleven different types, represented by British A to K, and their distribution covers the whole of south-east Britain, south and east of the Humber, Trent and Severn; the later issues, which Derek Allen dated from 70–60 BC onwards, appeared in the northerly part of this area. Once rulers started this practice, directly helped by the Gauls or not, it became a matter of tribal pride to follow.

GALLIC REFUGEES

In 58 BC we move on to firmer ground, for in this year Caesar began his campaign in Gaul and provides us with a valuable eyewitness who, with certain reservations, is reliable. The effect on Gaul was, of course, devastating: a great and large country of fierce independent tribes was reduced, after a long and bitter struggle, by total conquest, and shaped into a Roman province. The effect on Britain was much the same, although the full impact delayed. The immediate consequence was to precipitate migrations as Gauls fled from their homes to seek refuge and new life in Britain. In their train came the two large-scale raids by Caesar himself, who firmly stamped the seal of conquest, a formal act, to be ratified much later. The tracks of the Gallic refugees are seen by Warwick Rodwell in the distribution of the Gallo-Belgic coin type E, which is found in large numbers; about a hundred are scattered in an area round the coast from the Humber to Selsey Bill, in north Kent, north Essex and areas to the west. One of the most significant factors is the appearance of coin hoards, of which twelve are known, mostly in coastal areas. This burying of portable wealth in times of trouble could have resulted from waves of fleeing refugees faced with a hostile reception, or the actual invasion of Caesar. The period from 58 to 52 BC, when the conquest of Gaul was completed, was one of constant turmoil and upheaval, with bands of Gallic refugees making constant landfalls along the south and east coast and their reception could have varied considerably.

The distribution map of these coins[10] has a number of significant blank areas. Apart from a coastal hoard, there are only two coins in the territory of the Iceni; there is another gap north of the Thames which must represent the presence of the Catuvellauni; there is also an interesting spread on the north and western borders which could indicate Gallic penetration by the Trinovantes that the Catuvellauni may have been unable to prevent, but must have viewed with growing alarm. Among the refugees, we know from Caesar, were chiefs and their followers, like those of the Bellovaci, and who would have endeavoured to establish kingdoms for themselves if favourable areas could be found. The spread round the northern border of the Catuvellauni and the obvious new area of settlement on the south coast round Selsey Bill could be evidence of new kingdoms established by warrior aristocrats.

The evidence of pottery

This is the period when new types of pottery became evident, such as the famous Aylesford-Swarling series. In her full and careful analysis,[11] Ann Birchall places the introduction of this new and superior type of pottery around about the time of Caesar, and not earlier. It must be appreciated that the pottery comes from cemeteries where cremation burials are accompanied by rich grave goods, practices which were brought into Britain from Gaul. Furthermore, the Aylesford cemetery produced two gold coins, but not fortunately in as close association with the remains as one would wish. This was, after all, an excavation of 1890,[12] and, although the work of Arthur Evans was somewhat in advance of its day, it hardly compares with modern techniques. One of these coins is Gallo-Belgic E and the other British Q, considered to be a little later; if these are family burials, the cemetery would have continued in use long after the time of the initial settlement. These cemeteries in Kent clearly belong to new and wealthy settlers, who brought their potters and other craftsmen with them. The pottery they introduced into Britain are the first professionally made wares, remarkable in their fineness and elegance and obviously for use mainly as drinking vessels at the tables of the aristocrats. These newcomers have brought with them their addiction to wine, which they would have had little difficulty in obtaining in Gaul, where trade with the Mediterranean had been first established by the Greek colonists from as early as *c*. 600 BC.[13]

This brings us to another new and important piece of research carried out by David Peacock of Southampton University,[14] who has analysed the minerals in the clay, with which the wine containers or the amphorae were made. His conclusion is that a fair amount of wine was being brought into Britain from southern Italy from *c*. 50 BC which would fit very well with the sudden arrival here of groups of wealthy aristocrats from Gaul. Unfortunately, these large and heavy containers conformed to definite types, which were not subject to a great deal of change. Once a suitable form had been developed for ease of loading and transportation, there seemed no point in altering it. Thus one can find, even today, in the docks and shores of some parts of the Mediterranean heaps of *amphorae* which are very little different from those of two thousand years ago. Accepting the axiom that wine and the fine table wares must follow the newcomers, it must be assumed that these Italian *amphorae* will be found in these areas where they settled. The earliest type, pre-dating Caesar, is found at Hengistbury Head, a landfall near Christchurch, Hampshire, which has produced a great deal of evidence of continental visitors throughout the ages.[15] This little pocket of early wine connoisseurs remains an oddity, explicable to David Peacock only as trade directly with Italy. Another strange fact is that there are very few wine containers in Kent to go with the rich cemeteries. The greatest concentration is north of the Thames, on the border of the Catuvellauni and at Camulodunum. But this may be much later in the story and belong to a post-Caesarian Britain, as we will see below.

CAESAR'S EXPEDITIONS TO BRITAIN

So far the archaeological evidence has been difficult to interpret against the vague historical background. Caesar decided to invade Britain in 55 BC, and it is from his *Commentaries* that we have the first eyewitness account of our country. However, its serious limitations must be recognised: Caesar was only ever in contact with the peoples of the south-east which included the North Downs, the eastern tip of Kent, the Thames Estuary and, to a very limited extent, the land north of the Thames perhaps as far as St Albans and Hertford. His knowledge of the rest of the British Isles came from merchants who were probably reluctant to say much, as they wished to maintain good relationships with the Britons. Travellers' tales were as usual garbled and exaggerated, so he knew extremely little about the greater part of Britain.

The other factor to be considered in Caesar's Commentaries is the motive behind writing them. His account was not that of a keen-eyed scientific observer anxious to relay the marvels of a new land to an eager public like the travel books of today, but it was a political testament written to justify his actions. Caesar was writing for a particular audience, the Roman ruling class, which consisted of the senatorial order and their following. He was anxious to show this small powerful group that he was a brilliantly successful general, with his own special talent for speed and daring. Britain was merely a rung in the ladder of his rise to power. To consider this fully is beyond the scope of this book, since it would begin a detailed analysis of the confused and rapidly changing political scene at that time. In brief, Caesar had to convince his readers and listeners that Britain was a rich and important place, worthy of the attention of Rome in an expansive mood, and that his expedition was successful against great difficulties, the most formidable being the Ocean itself.

Caesar's account must, however, be studied carefully to see how much reliable evidence can be salvaged. Although he gives one of his reasons for the expedition as the help the Gauls had received from Britain, due to the close ties of kinship between them, he had to admit that the Gauls knew almost nothing about Britain. The Romans were ignorant of the equinoctial tide which wrecked their fleet in 55 BC and emboldened the Britons to renew their attack, which forced the Romans into a precipitate withdrawal. It is ironic that a failure of such dire proportions against the Britons and the elements was hailed in the Senate as such a remarkable achievement, that a public thanksgiving of twenty days was decreed.

The only useful information Caesar gives us in the account of the first expedition is about chariot fighting, which was so novel to him that his professional interest was aroused (see p. 29). The second venture of 54 BC was better organised and the Romans at least knew more about ocean tides. Scared of the large armada, the Britons retired inland to hold the first river crossing, which must have been near the Stour near Canterbury, since there is at Bigbury a strong Iron Age hill-fort, built, Caesar surmised, for inter-tribal war – now with entrances blocked by felled timbers. It must have been a shock to the Britons to see how rapidly and efficiently the legionaries dealt with such a stronghold. Having suffered serious damage to his fleet, this time from a violent storm, Caesar pauses in his account to give his readers a description of Britain. But this was clearly added at a later date, and almost entirely taken from other writers.

If one examines Caesar's two raids objectively from the military point of view, they were rash in conception, hasty and ill-advised in execution – in fact almost a total disaster. Nor is the taint of failure concealed by Caesar's *bravura* style. Historians have not only accepted Caesar wholeheartedly, but his entry into Britain has become established in the lay mind as the beginning of the Roman occupation. This is probably due also to the choice of the Commentaries as a work set for Latin prose examinations. Older generations with a classical education remembered their Caesar, but knew very little about the real conquest of Roman Britain, since Tacitus, a more difficult text, was not in the syllabus. The impact of Caesar on Britain was slight, certainly in area and probably on the peoples themselves. After a generation or so, he would have been hardly a credible folk memory. It is even possible that the Britons regarded it as a victory for themselves, since the Romans left so hurriedly and were not seen again for almost a hundred years. The grim realities of the war – the iron will, discipline and power of the legions – were unpleasant aspects soon erased by the mind's delicate balance. The stories sung by the bards would have been those of British heroes battling with the iron-clad monsters.

In the main narrative we now have a name, Cassivellaunus, the chief commander appointed by the Britons to lead their defence against Rome. He was the king of a tribe north of the Thames, and had been at war previously with the other tribes. Although the name of his tribe is not stated, it was most probably the Catuvellauni. Caesar forced the Thames crossing and the Britons then realised that their only chance of survival was by avoiding pitched battles and using guerrilla tactics to draw the Romans into the interior, further away from their base. At this stage Caesar introduces an ally, a young prince, Mandubracius, who had come to him as a suppliant prior to the invasion, having fled when his father who was the King of the Trinovantes, had been killed by Cassivellaunus. Caesar sent the prince back to his tribe as their king, under Roman protection, having exacted hostages and corn. The result was that five other tribes – the Cenimagni (presumably the Iceni), the Segontiaci, the Ancalites, the Bibroci and the Cassi – not only surrendered to Caesar, but told him where he could find the stronghold of Cassivellaunus. A claim for this site was made by Mortimer Wheeler at Wheathamstead, near St Albans, but the identification is by no means sure. The names of four of these tribes offer no guide of their situation, but presumably they were enemies of the Catuvellauni and lived on the north or western borders. If this is the case, they could have been of recent Gallic origin.

The British king then tried another tactic, and ordered the Kentish tribes to attack Caesar's base. This incident gives us the name of four of their kings – Cingetorix, Carvilius, Taximagulus and Segovax – and another, Lugotorix, who was captured, all names with a strong Gallic flavour. But this attempt failed and Cassivellaunus was forced to surrender under terms imposed by Caesar, who was now anxious to get back to Gaul before the winter. Caesar could thus claim a success, for he had defeated the chief ruler and imposed terms which included an annual tribute. It is also possible that some of the hostages, men of noble birth, were sent to Rome. As far as the Senate was concerned, Britain had been conquered, and all that remained was for it to be officially taken over and made into a Roman province. But the great revolt in Gaul, culminating in the stubborn resistance organised by Vercingetorix, prevented Caesar from having any further interest in Britain. After this the civil wars caused the Romans to forget such a slight and distant problem.

COMMIUS OF THE ATREBATES

There is one more incident of this period to relate which has an important bearing on pre-Roman Britain. It concerns Commius, king of the Atrebates, a tribe north of the Seine and near the coast. After Caesar's conquest of this area he had made him king of this tribe and had a high regard of him. Such was Caesar's estimates of his capabilities as a diplomat, that he sent him to Britain before the invasion with the purpose of trying to win over some of the tribes to Rome. It is likely that the tribes Caesar had in mind were those who had fled from Gaul at his approach. The Bellovaci were near-neighbours of the Atrebates and Caesar clearly hoped to divide these Gallo-Belgic peoples from the indigenous tribes of Britain. Commius, however, failed at the outset and was taken prisoner the moment he disembarked on the shores of Kent and announced his mission. He was handed back to Caesar after the landing and the battle which followed (IV, 27). Commius had been accompanied by thirty horsemen and this may have created some suspicions about his real intent. Commius went with Caesar on his second invasion and helped with the peace negotiations (V, 22). After the revolt of the Menapii, a tribe in the Low Countries, near the mouth of the Rhine, Commius was called into service to garrison the area with his cavalry (VI, 6).

In spite of all this and the favoured treatment his tribe had received from the Romans, Commius threw in his lot with Vercingetorix contributing 4,000 troops from his tribe, and persuaded the Bellovaci, against their better judgment, to send 2,000. Commius was appointed one of the chief officers of the Gallic host. After Caesar's great victory over Vercingetorix, Commius survived to continue the struggle (VIII, 6) and even successfully sought help from the Germans. It was with their aid that he finally escaped from the battle. Caesar sent a special posse of centurions to execute him, but after receiving a severe head wound he managed to escape, resolving that he would never again set his eyes on a Roman (VIII, 23). He avoided yet another encounter with a party sent after him, and, after this, decided to sail to Britain with a band of his followers. Even then he was almost captured, as Frontinus related in one of his *Strategems* (II, 13, 11): since his boat was becalmed in the absence of any wind, he foiled the pursuing Romans by hoisting his sails and giving the impression he was away and out of reach.

The territory he won for himself in Britain was named after his own people, the Atrebates, and was centred upon Silchester. It did not become, however, an area of wealth measured in terms of luxury goods and amphorae, comparable to that north of the Thames. Commius gained and maintained his dynasty by means of the sword and his strong personality.

3

Britain between the Invasions
54 BC–AD 43

The terms imposed on the Britons by Caesar were hostages, an annual tribute and a direction to Cassivellaunus to leave Mandubracius and the Trinovantes in peace. Britain had now been opened up to Roman trade and influence to a much greater extent than before, and the effect of this may be measured by the scale of imports, such as metalware, glass, pottery, above all wine from Italy. David Peacock[1] dates his early amphorae forms, i.e. the variant of Dressel 1B, roughly from *c.* 70 to *c.* 10 BC and his distribution pattern is highly significant (Fig. 2)[2]. There are two concentrations, Hampshire with eight, as mentioned above, while the area north of the Thames has over twenty examples. The distribution of these early Italian *amphorae* poses problems; for example, there are more in Britain than the whole of north-west Gaul, but they appear in the Upper Rhine and in Central Gaul. Obviously the trade route is not across the Channel, and this is true also of the imported pottery of a slightly later date (see p. 42 below).

The growing wealth of the Gallo-Belgic rulers can also be seen in the new coin types, known as British L and M, which are much superior to all the earlier issues and imply the presence of specialist die-cutters, probably sent from Rome under the general cover of technical assistance, which may have been written into any treaty. These coins also show a definite spread of infiltration to the north-west beyond the Icknield Way. An explanation may be sought in the alliances Caesar made in Britain. The kings of Kent without exception had been hostile: they had seized Commius at the very outset of his diplomatic mission, and had only made peace overtures when thoroughly beaten. The tribute Caesar levied would have fallen on these tribes who had resisted, and the Catuvellauni and the people of North Kent would have been forced to pay. This may account for the virtual absence of early *amphorae* in their areas. But Caesar was always generous to those who aided him. How the Trinovantes and their kindred benefited economically is difficult to judge, but it was for the Romans an opportunity for consolidating their influence in a critical area of Britain. The effect is dramatic and shows the extent of Gallo-Belgic territory on the northern borders of the Catuvellauni, with Welwyn as the main centre and Braughing a subsidiary. It is clear also that the kingdom of Commius is cut off from any contact with Rome and this is consistent with his vow. The trade in Hampshire is an entirely separate issue, since there is no suggestion that these people were in contact with Caesar, but they had their own trade relationship directly with the Mediterranean.[3]

It was not a state of affairs which could last very long. The Catuvellauni smarted under their defeat and the ascendancy of the newcomers on their north and western borders, who were now prospering under the beneficence of Rome. But Rome had a long arm and an overt act against her too soon might produce swift and unpleasant consequences. While Caesar was still alive and powerful, the Britons were forced to keep quiet, but with his assassination in 44, and the widespread civil war which followed, a great change took place.

An additional element to help us with the historical narrative is the new habit of the British rulers to include their names on coins. Although it has produced some difficult problems, one could not even begin to sort out the dynastic connections and changes without this evidence. The first king to do this was Addedomaros, and the distribution of his coins indicates that he was a ruler of the Trinovantes, a successor to Mandubracius. It would appear also that his centre of power moved from the Braughing area to Camulodunum, but whether this was due to conquest or dynastic marriage is not possible to deduce, but the collection of small tribes now appears to have been brought under a single ruler, Tasciovanus, with his centre of power now at Verulamium. This clearly indicates the extent of his large kingdom which he ruled under the title *ricomus*, the Celtic equivalent of the Latin *rex*. Evidence suggests that the tribe was now beginning to move against its northern neighbours, since Welwyn is only ten miles from Verulamium. Perhaps Addedomaros was forced to move to the west; if so, this event must be dated after *c.* 40–30 BC, although Professor Frere has placed it much later at the time of the serious defeat of the Roman army on the Rhine in 17 BC.

Coin issues of Tasciovanus are considerable and of great complexity, and clearly belong to a long reign, but the distribution pattern of each issue show such fluctuations that it is difficult to read a coherent story into them at present. There are two issues which have the mint name CAMV, and this is interpreted as a conquest of the Trinovantian capital, but this was of short duration, since all the coins placed in the latter part of his reign have no mint mark, or are from Verulamium; furthermore, the distribution does not include Camulodunum. At the peak of his career, which comes early in his reign, the coins of Tasciovanus spread south of the Thames and to the north-west. It may mean that, as a young and energetic ruler, he had striking

Fig. 2   Extent of Gallo-Belgic influence at the time of Caesar, excluding the settlements i
Kent and that of Commius

success in overrunning the Trinovantes and their kindred folk on his borders and even establishing some control over tribes in the south, but that soon his new empire crumbled, although he managed to hold a much enlarged kingdom at the expense of the Gallic peoples to his north. Other names like DIAS, RVES, SEGO appear on his late coins, which may suggest he was now sharing power with others, and seems finally to have been succeeded by a man whose name begins ANDOCO . . . with the same coin spread as that late in the reign of the old king, with a possible expansion to the west.[5]

The next ruler to command attention is Dubnovellaunos, but the problem here is that his coins are found in two quite separate areas, that of the Trinovantes and north-east Kent, with very little overlap, and there is no relationship between the two series. Those from Camulodunum closely follow the style of Addedomaros, and here he can be seen as the successor, whereas the Kent series based on Canterbury, are different, but appear to be contemporary with Tasciovanus. Some, including Warwick Rodwell, argue for two different people, but this seems an unnecessary complication. If he followed Addedomaros at Camulodunum, he may have been responsible for the ejection of Tasciovanus after his brief conquest. In this great struggle between the two main contenders – the Britons and the Gallic kings – one can understand why Dubnovellaunus needed to counter the expansion of Trinovantian-Catuvellaunian power south of the Thames, by seizing the kingdom of East Kent. This would have given him control of the whole of the north of the Thames Estuary, now vital for trade with Gaul. One may even see the hand of Augustus in this; there had been from time to time the idea of completing the conquest of Caesar, as is apparent from C.E. Stevens' brilliant analysis of contemporary Roman thinking.[6]

That skilled and far-sighted statesman, Augustus, would have built up alliances with all those forces in Britain which had pro-Roman leanings. Of these, the Gallic bloc of the Trinovantes and their associates was the most important. Augustus would have been at pains to maintain the links forged by Caesar, and one must also appreciate the crucial need to ensure a safe landing place and base, which made the control of East Kent, by a Roman ally, a constant factor throughout. As will be seen later, Augustus had also won over an ally in Tincommius of the Atrebates, as part of a plan to enclose the Catuvellauni. Although Rome may have been preoccupied when Tasciovanus embarked on his grand scheme of a conquest, this would have caused Augustus to consider the urgent need for a counterbalance. Dubnovellaunus was probably a ruler acting under Roman advice and economic pressure. This could have been happening in 27 BC when, according to Cassius Dio, Augustus was in Gaul with an invasion very much in mind. But he was suddenly diverted by serious trouble developing in Spain, which absorbed his attention in 26 BC and must have given him second thoughts about Britain.

There is another piece of evidence which adds to the picture. Stevens argues from a reference of Horace, the Court poet, that by 15 BC some tribes in Britain had a 'relationship' with Rome which could be interpreted in treaty terms. The Greek geographer Strabo in his account of Britain[7] tells us that certain British rulers had set up offerings in the Capitol; this usually implies the ratification of formal treaties; but the problem is the date of this statement. It is difficult to place it as early as this, and some, including Professor Frere, would put it after the death of Augustus in AD 14.[8] If so, it must refer to a totally different situation, a strong argument for which is that there is no mention in the *Res Gestae* of Augustus, an important document in which the Emperor recorded all those acts by which he wished to be remembered. It took the form of a large inscription carved on monuments erected all over the Empire, but the only example to survive, with its text in an extensive form, is that found at Ankara and known as the *Monumentum Ancyranum*. What this remarkable inscription does tell us, however, is that there were two British kings Dubnovellaunus and another, whose name began TIN . . . , which can only be Tincommius, who had appeared in Rome as suppliants presumably after they had fled from their kingdoms. The accepted date of this monument is AD 7, which means that this event must be dated before this. As we shall see, it fits with the sudden rise of Cunobelinus and his conquest of the Trinovantes, which can now be narrowly assigned to a year or so *c*. AD 1. To summarise, the evidence points to a flurry of diplomatic activity by Augustus in 17 BC prior to a projected invasion, which could be linked with the sudden rise of Dubnovellaunus and the spread of Roman control over the Thames Estuary, and the equally sudden reversal *c*. AD 1 when Cunobelinus seized power and the Catuvellauni took over.

Against this, one has to assess the significance of recent work by Clive Partridge at Skeleton Green, near Braughing. His excavation has produced a remarkable assemblage of pottery and metalwork imported from Italy and Gaul. It includes over 100 lid-seated jars in a mica-dusted ware from north Italy, which may have been containers, and almost 100 vessels from the Arretine factory, as well as small colour-coated drinking cups. Not only does this seem to be the result of normal trade, but, as with the Dressel IB *amphorae*, a direct transmission of goods from Italy into Hertford-shire, perhaps along a route via Marseilles up the Rhône and down the Rhine.[9] The vessels include *mortaria*, kitchen wares with heavy bowls and a pouring spout, used for pulverising and mixing food – a method peculiar to the Roman kitchen. The Britons, however Gallic in origin, could hardly have adopted this practice in such a traditional domestic area as the kitchen, merely through trading contacts. The presence of these vessels must, therefore, indicate the existence of a small community of Romanised people in Hertfordshire preparing meals in their customary way. The suggestion of a trading post seems the most likely. If there was one here, others must surely have existed elsewhere, especially in the area of Camulodunum or near the point of entry in the Colne river or its estuary. The evidence from the pottery and metalwork suggests a date bracket of 10 BC–15 AD, but there are already indications that further work on and near the site could widen this.

Although it is unwise to leap to any implications arising out of this new evidence, it would seem to present a paradox. If the sudden rise of Cunobelinus is seen as a set-back to the Roman policy of maintaining allies in the key coastal areas, how can this be equated with the appearance of a Roman trading settlement at Braughing in the years which followed? Or was Cunobelinus as anti-Roman as some have assumed on the basis of the old hostility between the Catuvellauni, the earlier settlers, and the more recent migrants from Gaul?

CUNOBELINUS

Cunobelinus does indeed present some difficult problems. It is not clear who he was, or where he came from, but his rise to power was rapid and dramatic. The facts, based on the existence of his coins, so brilliantly studied by Derek Allen, show beyond doubt that, as soon as he gained power over the Catuvellauni, he moved against the Trinovantes. Since his earliest issues are minted at Camulodunum,[10] one wonders even if he was a Catuvellaunian exile and seized the throne in a palace revolt. Some of the early issues portray a victory with a palm or laurel wreath, a motif borrowed from the Romans which leaves in no doubt that Cunobelinus was celebrating a victory. It is also significant that the very fine series of his gold staters were all minted at Camulodunum, clearly indicating the centre of his power from the very beginning. All this worries Warwick Rodwell, who even suggests that the affiliation to Tasciovanus is a deliberate falsification to claim a right to Catuvellaunian territory. But who would that deceive? Certainly not the Catuvellauni.

The circumstances of his dramatic coup may be obscure. It must be seen against the preoccupation of Augustus with Germany.[11] It was at this time that Rome had serious hopes of conquering and holding a great tract of land up to the Elbe. There had been a continuous series of campaigns, initiated by Drusus and continued up to his accidental death in 9 BC and then by Tiberius in AD 4, with solid achievements. The critical campaign against the Marcomanni under their leader Maroboduus would, if successful, have added Bohemia, but it had to be broken off almost at the point of victory in AD 6 by the great revolt in Pannonia, which demanded the immediate presence of Tiberius in that area. Instead of a crushing victory, Rome had to be content with a treaty with Maroboduus. Rome's position in Germany now seemed secure: consolidation and integration into the Roman provincial system was the next stage.

It was here that Augustus made one of his rare errors of judgment. The man he selected for this task was a sound administrator and well versed in the law, but he was no military commander. Another deciding factor was undoubtedly that Quinctilius Varus was married to the great-niece of the Emperor, who was always anxious to keep political power in the family. The Roman secret service was also at fault, since they did not know enough about Arminius, Chief of the Cherusci. He had been courted by Rome and given equestrian status, presumably with a handsome grant. But, instead of being a friend in an important area, he was drawing the tribes into a conspiracy against Rome, playing on their fears as the Druids were to do in Britain. He invited Varus to his home on the Weser, midway between the Elbe and the Rhine, but when the legate retired westwards with his three legions to their winter quarters, Arminius ambushed him in the forests of the Barenau area, somewhere near modern Osnabrück, and totally destroyed the Roman force – a disaster of unparalleled magnitude.

For Augustgus, the *clades Variana* of AD 9 was a serious trauma, causing an instant and continued withdrawal from his mind of any further imperial ambitions. One can readily understand that in the first decade of the first century, Augustus and his close advisers were too preoccupied with these events to pay much attention to disturbances in Britain. Cunobelinus must have known that he could act without any serious threat of Roman reprisals. His political astuteness may have prompted him into giving an assurance that the balance of power was not seriously affected, and that Roman traders were still welcome in Camulodunum and elsewhere north of the Thames.

The extent of his kingdom is also a matter of dispute. It is not clear if the distribution of coins represents political power or actual trade between the British tribes with a currency which could buy imports, all assisted by the spreading influence of capitalism. The scatter of his coins in north Kent and Oxfordshire may merely indicate a spread of commerce, especially as there are no obvious points of concentration. From the outset, one of the chief motifs on his coins was the ear of barley, derived originally from the disintegrated wreath of Apollo of the stater of Philip of Macedon. C. E. Stevens made a delightful play on this in comparing it with the vine leaf in the coins of Verica,[12] who became king of the Atrebates *c.* AD 10, as an allusion to British beer being better than imported wine. But this is far too fanciful and belied by the great quantity of amphorae at Camulodunum during this period. It certainly was an emblem, not of beer, but of the great wealth in corn he was determined to develop under his long and peaceful rule. Cunobelinus must have realised that, to pursue this policy of economic development in a stable community, he would have to come to terms with his 'Gallic' neighbours and with Rome. This, as we have seen, may have come earlier than his last series of gold coins, which show such an unmistakable Roman influence. The extraordinary range of motifs used on his coins and their significance would make a fascinating and rewarding study with the interweaving of Celtic and classical themes. This brings us to the closing years of his reign, when Rome was able to increase its diplomatic pressure;

but before we follow this development, one needs to look more closely at the British capital itself.

CAMULODUNUM

Between the River Colne and its southern tributary the Roman River, and the stream to the north known as Salary Brook, there is a large area of over 70 square kilometres surrounded by defence earthworks, known as dykes, which are basically to prevent chariots breaking through. Over the years several archaeologists (the most prominent of whom has been Professor C. F. C. Hawkes) have been plotting and studying them and above all, attempting to work out a rational chronological development; but there is still much to be done. The latest effort by Warwick Rodwell divides the dykes into six main periods[13] and the point which stands out is that the original centre of the complex is not the Roman *colonia* where Colchester now stands, but at Gosbecks, where a large religious centre with a temple theatre has been found. Somewhere to the north-east must be the British capital and this idea is supported by the discovery of a Roman fort nearby. It was only in Rodwell's phase 4 that an area north of the Colne is defended, and this helps to explain why so little structural evidence and native occupation were found in the Sheepen site to the east of the Roman *colonia*.[14] The answers to many of our problems must be in the large area between Colchester and the Roman River.

THE ATREBATES

Before continuing with the story, one must look back to Commius and the Atrebates. The kingdom he created after his flight from Gaul *c*. 50 BC can only be defined by the distribution of the coinage he initiated, a distinctive type known as British Q, on the reverse of which was a triple-tailed horse. The spread is wide, some north of the Thames in the Colne Valley, others covering much of Hampshire and Sussex, with a concentration on the coast round Selsey Bill, an area which, as we have seen above, had evidence of earlier Gallic settlement. It looks as if Commius was powerful enough to assert his authority over a very large area, although the twelve known coins which actually bear his name do not extend so far to the north or west. He was succeeded, *c*. 20 BC, by his son Tincommius, whose coins have much the same distribution. As stated above, Augustus scored a great diplomatic triumph in winning over this son of the man who had hated the Romans so vehemently.

The alliance was marked by new coinage copying Roman *denarii*. Although the choice was a little odd, the dies must have been cut by a Roman diecutter. In one example (Mack 96),[15] the die has a strong resemblance to a much earlier issue of 82–81 BC struck by the moneyer Publius Crepusius, showing a horseman hurling a spear (Sydenham No. 378);[16] another bears an eagle with wings displayed (Mack 105), based possibly on *denarii* of *c.* 68 and 37 BC (Sydenham Nos. 809 and 1150); another, a galloping bull (Mack 106 cf. Sydenham 743, without Europa). This raises the intriguing speculation: how were the choices of types made by Tincommius? Was he shown a collection of Roman silver *denarii*? One at least of the coins had the letters CA, which is possibly Calleva. If so, it shows that this was the centre selected by Tincommius for his capital, in preference to the primary Gallic settlement at Selsey Bill. This may be related to the subsequent division of this large kingdom into two parts, the Atrebates and the Regni.

Some time before AD 7 Tincommius, as we have seen above, was driven out of his kingdom to appear before Augustus as a suppliant king. His expulsion may not have been caused by external forces, but was probably the result of a family row, since he was succeeded by Eppillus, who also claimed to be a son of Commius; Calleva remained the mint and the motifs continued in the Roman tradition, even to the extent of the use of the Latin *rex* to denote Eppillus' status. The balance of power was not affected, but what is interesting is that most of his coins have been found in east Kent. From the small number of his coins in Atrebatian territory, it can be argued that his reign here was short and that he in turn was driven out by Verica, another son or, by now more likely, a grandson of Commius, in yet another palace upheaval. Eppillus was successful in gaining control of east Kent following the appearance of Cunobelinus at Camulodunum and the confusion caused by the flight of Dubnovellaunus from Camulodunum. This can be dated to before AD 7 as Dubnovellaunus is listed with his fellow exile on the *Res Gestae* of Augustus. The final king who may have played a part in this family drama is Epaticcus, a son of Tasciovanus. His coins, not a great number, appear only among the Atrebates. He could have expelled Eppillus after a short reign, to have been removed in turn by Verica.

By this time it must have become obvious to the Britons that the threat of a Roman invasion had diminished almost to vanishing point, and this was the view that was now accepted in Rome.

THE ICENI

Little so far has been said about the tribe which initiated the Revolt and who occupied much of East Anglia. Much less is known of the Iceni than of the tribes in the South-East which can now be seen, although vaguely, in a historical context through the classical sources, their coins and the imports of wine, metalware and pottery. The Iceni belong to earlier folk movements from Belgium and Holland across the North Sea, making a landfall on the Wash or on the Norfolk rivers, the Waveney and the Yare. The date of this migration was round about 500 BC and these people brought with them knowledge of iron smelting and appear to have settled down peaceably with the indigenous inhabitants.

About 450 BC another migration took place in the form of bands of aristocratic warriors from the Marne Valley, looking for territories with people to conquer and rule. Some of the earliest fortifications seem to date from this event, showing that the inhabitants were not prepared to surrender without a struggle. But the new warriors, with their desperate need for land and their superiority in warfare – with their fine iron swords and light chariots – soon overran East Anglia, as they did Lincolnshire and east Yorkshire,[17] and established kingdoms which they ruled as an aristocratic minority. They brought with them their metal workers in bronze and iron, and produced weapons and accoutrements far superior to anything yet seen in Britain. Some of these objects have been ploughed up in recent years, like the famous Snettisham treasure in 1948[18] and 1950, including a remarkable gold torc which had a Gallic quarter-stater inside one terminal; another from Sedgeford in 1965,[19] two miles away, and five from Ipswich in 1968.[20] Most of these objects are connected with horses and chariots and typical of the wargear sported by the Marnian chieftains. From the quality of their expensive gear and gold objects found in their territories, it may be considered that the Iceni were a wealthy people and that their leaders were primarily interested in horses – a suggestion which may have some bearing on later events.

Thanks to recent archaeological discoveries, mainly through the ploughing of new ground and deeper ploughing, we know now more about the Iceni.[21] However, the historical sources do not help to clarify the picture very much and they seem to stand outside the great dynastic struggles to the south. There is also no evidence of any deep penetration of Roman traders before the conquest (Fig. 2). The tribe is included in Caesar's list of the peoples who sought an alliance with Rome when he was engaged with the Catuvellauni, and, as we have already seen, it is likely that some of the other tribes, otherwise unknown, may have occupied the northern boundary of the Catuvellauni. On this basis one could visualise a kind of northern bloc of pro-Roman tribes which Roman diplomacy strove to maintain. Apart from this single piece of evidence we have to rely entirely on a study of the coins of the tribe, and fortunately once more we have the invaluable help of Derek Allen.[22] His distribution map clearly shows the extent of their territory: it did not stretch much further south than the watershed of the Lark, as far in fact as a line between modern Bury St Edmunds and Ipswich on the Orwell (Fig. 1).

The first coins were minted *c.* 10 BC and were from a type of Tasciovanus. But the Iceni soon developed their own personal motif, which is an animal sometimes looking like a boar and at other times like a horse (referred to as the Boar-Horse types). In the end the horse became the predominant animal, which may reflect one of the main interests of the tribal aristocracy. As in other British tribes, Roman influence is clearly detectable and this appears in a head surrounded by a laurel wreath copied from a *denarius* of 58 BC (Sydenham 915). The first name to appear is a ruler Antedios, whom Allen thought contemporary with Addedomaros (*c.* 15–10 BC). There is another type which actually bears the tribal name ECENI, a practice not followed by any other British tribe. Two other names probably of kings are abbreviated to AESV and SAEMV. It is possible, as Allen has suggested, that the different names and types of coin may represent division in the tribe, although the distribution patterns do not help in defining them; what, however, emerges is that there is a main centre of wealth in the Freckenham–Lakenheath area rather than the later Icenian capital near Norwich. The site of the royal residence should be sought therefore in the Breckland area. This idea is certainly supported by rich finds of gold and other artefacts of other metals.[23]

When an attempt is made to establish a basic chronology of the tribal coinage difficulties arise. To fit a period of the unlettered series into an early sequence, it is necessary to place Antedios after *c.* AD 25 which would have made him a contemporary of Cunobelinus. Then follow the coins with the tribal name and the other two rulers, whom Derek Allen places among the last of the issues. From this we draw the interesting conclusion that they overlap into the post-Conquest period. But here the question to be asked is; would the Roman government allow tribal issues within the Province even in a client kingdom? If so, where are coins of Prasutagus the client king himself, and of Cogidubnus, the client king of the Regni? The fact that these Icenian coins appear in hoards with Roman coins, the one from Santon Downham, as late as Claudius, does not necessarily bring their mint date into the post-Conquest period. There could still be quantities in general use and even buried as late as the Revolt.[24]

There remains one issue which is very odd indeed and it is a very great pity that Derek Allen did not have time to develop his ideas about it; but at least he left a note in manuscript form which has now been published.[25] There are only five coins known of this type, and a careful study has produced a reasonable version of two legends, one on the obverse reads SVBIPPASTO and another on the reverse – ESICOFECIT. Taking the latter first, this seems to give us the name of a moneyer – ESICO who minted the coins and used the Latin verb FECIT. What does SVBIPPASTO mean on the other side? The prefix SVB could signify 'under' but the name is very unlikely unless, as Derek Allen has suggested, it is a mistake for PRASTO. This has been confirmed by a study of four more coins by H.K. Mossop who has found on one of them the letter R after SVB which offers an expansion to R(ICON) PRASTO which could mean 'under Prasutagus'.

POST-AUGUSTUS POLICIES AND TRADE

Augustus bequeathed to Tiberius a policy of *status quo*, an instruction not to attempt to expand the Empire. This policy the new emperor, made weary by many years of frustration and denigration, was only too anxious to accept. By now Cunobelinus may have signed a formal treaty with Rome and this could be implied from Strabo if one accepts the view that his famous statement dated to *c.* AD 14. This states that, with important export duties, Rome received greater profit than any army could produce, and then he listed the British exports as grain, cattle, gold, silver, iron, hides, slaves and hunting dogs, in return for trinkets and ivory, ornaments, amber and glass, in terms of real wealth, an imbalance reminiscent of Victorian colonisation in Africa. Strabo curiously enough does not include wine, which by now had reached considerable proportions.[26] It certainly reflects the Roman attitude towards Britain at this time and it is, in effect, an apology for the delay in implementing Caesar's conquest, arguing that the treaties now completed make the Roman position in Britain so secure that there is no longer any need for Rome to invade.

During the campaigns on the Rhine under Germanicus in AD 16, some troop ships were blown across the North Sea and wrecked on the British coast. These were returned, clearly indicating a friendly gesture from one of the tribes, perhaps under a treaty obligation. Apart from Cunobelinus and the Iceni, a probable candidate is, as we have seen, Verica, who claimed kinship with Commius, and may have been a grandson; he succeeded or took over from Eppillus *c.* AD 10. The second main coin issue of Verica bears the title REX, and among his later issues there are coins with a head modelled on a portrait of Tiberius.

There is much work to be done on the artefacts brought into Britain before the Conquest, as will be apparent from the evidence from Skeleton Green. We have a great deal to learn about the pottery and it is only in the last few years that students have been specialising with profit on the identification and distribution of imported wares.[27] Similar studies are now needed on the metalwork. The problem is that of distinguishing the fine bronzes made in Britain from those of continental smiths, especially in the case of brooches. One can perhaps be on surer ground with silver objects, but there are very few of these. The best finds of this nature come from burials where a chief is laid out with his personal adornments and drinking cups for use in the next world. There are graves like this at Welwyn; one of the most interesting was found in 1965 in excavating trenches for gas mains on the Panshanger housing estate. This sad story and the subsequent rescue of so much useful material and evidence is told by Ian Stead in his report.[28] This rich burial contained five complete Dressel type IB *amphorae*, a fascinating collection of imported pottery, a complete set of twenty-four glass gaming pieces in four colours, probably made in northern Italy and two-handled silver cups dated to *c.* 25–0 BC, and quite certainly of Mediterranean origin. There was also a bronze wine strainer, a curiously shaped bronze dish or tray, fragments of fittings from an elaborate

D

wooden box and a triangular iron knife which may have been for cutting leather. Similar graves have been found at Welwyn in road works in 1906,[29] but are ill-recorded: there were two silver cups found in one burial, and from another an imported bronze bowl. The most famous finds from these discoveries were the fire dogs, which one can now see in the British Museum.

Dr Stead's report is also useful in bringing together the evidence from a number of other similar burials and in providing a review of their chronology, from which it is evident that the Welwyn groups are the earliest and fit well into the new pottery evidence from Skeleton Green dating to the second half of the first century BC. They form the nucleus of a wealthy group of Gallic migrants who settled here as a result of Caesar's activities in Gaul, but who were also able to maintain trading links with Italy and the Mediterranean. In the light of this sophistication it is perhaps not surprising that their descendants gained from Claudius municipal honours for their town at Verulamium.

One must also consider the important burial in Lexden Park, near Colchester, excavated by Philip Laver in 1924.[30] This is a large burial mound about 80 feet in diameter, demolished to make way for housing. As a rescue operation Laver cut a trench into the centre and removed the burial pit in the shape of a rough oval 30 feet by 18 feet, but he did not examine the rest of the mound. The burial had been very much disturbed and all the objects of precious metal removed. An iron bound chest had been smashed to pieces and its contents taken. The collection of objects recovered, although in a poor condition, are interesting for their Roman associations. The most crucial object for dating the burial is a small medallion of Augustus, which on careful examination was found to be an actual *denarius* of the Emperor of a type issued in 17 BC. The bust had been cut out, soldered on to a silver disc and put into a moulded frame. As the report indicates, it is very similar to the portrait of Tiberius mounted on a legionary sword scabbard found at Mainz, and now in the British Museum.[31] This is probably a sword presented to an officer who served in the campaigns in Germany under Germanicus. There are no other fragments in the grave which would have come from such a scabbard, although there are pieces of a mail coat decorated with silver studs and with bronze hinges, identical to those found on legionary armour at a later date. The Romans copied this type of armour (*lorica hamata*) from the Celts, the finest example being that on the young warrior in the Musée Calvet in Avignon.[32] Iron fragments appear to suggest a large and elaborate funeral palanquin on which the body was carried and placed in the tomb. Other bronze objects – a small table, a pedestal, a cupid, a foot and the fittings including a pair of hinges of a palmette form and pieces of embossed plates – are all Roman imports. There is also a fine boar, a sitting bull and a remarkable head of a griffin on a curved mount, as if from a large flagon, all of which would well repay careful study. Fascinating too are the pieces of fine gold thread which must have been woven into the shroud, or perhaps a fine linen cloth to cover the face.

The question arises as to the identity of this warrior buried in such style at Camulodunum. Can he be linked with an historical character? He had received gifts connecting him with Augustus some time after 17 BC. But the *amphorae* of Dressel form I provide a later date at the end of the first century BC. Cunobelinus, who died *c.* 40 AD, would seem to be almost too late.

THE DEATH OF CUNOBELINUS AND ITS AFTERMATH

The final years of this great king, who had truly been called *Britannorum rex* by Suetonius,[33] was marred by a family upset, which led to the expulsion from Britain of his son Adminius. This happened when Gaius (Caligula) was reviewing his troops in Germany in AD 39 or 40. Suetonius records the arrival of the banished prince with a group of his followers. This prompted the unbalanced Emperor to send a despatch to Rome announcing the surrender of the whole of Britain. Subsequently he seemed to be planning an invasion to occupy his new province; but he decided to have a triumph instead. His assassins, however, had other plans.

It has been generally agreed that the same ruler, although with slightly different spelling, is represented by four British coins, two of which bear the letters AM, another AMMI and the fourth the name in full AMMINVS, with the further letters DVN on the reverse, which is probably *dunum*, the Celtic word for a fort, referring to the capital where the coins were minted. The distribution pattern is not very helpful: the find-spots of two are unknown, another was found on the Roman fort on Waddon Hill, Dorset, and has therefore travelled, and the fourth was recovered from Castle Hill Camp, Folkestone. Derek Allen considered the types to be Kentish and suggests that Adminius ruled probably the north-eastern part of Kent on behalf of his father a short time before his death.[34] In his closing years the old king may have become enfeebled, or there may have been trouble over the succession.

There were two other sons we know about, Togodumnus and Caratacus, the latter especially thirsting for power. The precise date of the death of Cunobelinus is not certain, but it must be within a year of AD 40, either before or immediately after Caratacus struck out on his own south of the Thames, while Togodumnus, presumably the eldest son, inherited the kingdom. The flight of Adminius may be connected with these events and perhaps Caratacus was to take over Kent. But he was not content with this, since another king is soon seeking Roman protection – this time Verica of the Atrebates. The Atrebates had a claim to east Kent through Eppillus who had reigned there from *c.* AD 5 to 20 until Cunobelinus had gained control. The Catuvellaunian ruling house also remembered Epaticcus, an uncle of Cunobelinus, who had established himself over the Atrebates, but was soon banished or killed by Verica. There was obviously much latent and even overt hostility between the two ruling houses, but Cunobelinus chose to accept the position because Verica had a treaty relationship to Rome: when he was powerful enough to challenge this, he could no longer be sure that Rome might not react. He may also himself have been under a solemn obligation to Rome to respect this treaty in any arrangement of his own.

With the incapacity or death of the old king, the whole position was changed. Caratacus hoped to succeed where Epaticcus had failed and to gain control of the whole of the territories south of the Thames and forge them into his kingdom. What we know of the historical background seems to imply this. But the evidence is rather thin, consisting only of two identical silver coins bearing the letters CARA (Mack No. 265), one of which was found near Guildford. The significant point about this issue is that it is a copy of the type minted by Epaticcus, and could be taken as evidence of the claim Caratacus felt he had to the Atrebatic kingdom.

There is further evidence of the expansion of Catuvellaunian power from a statement by Dio Cassius in his *Roman History*. This gives us the only account of the Roman invasion of AD 43. Soon after the landing the commander Aulus Plautius received the surrender of a part of the Dobunni, who, he adds, were subjects of the Catuvellauni.[35] The Dobunnic coin issues seem to indicate two different series bearing the names Corio and Bodvoc, with distributions in the south-west and north-east respectively. It is generally assumed that it was the north-east half of the tribe which was under Catuvellaunian influence. This is confirmed by the spread of coins of Cunobelinus up the Thames into the eastern territory of the tribe, but there are very few beyond this and only one coin, that of Epaticcus, of the Catuvellaunian dynasty itself at Bagendon, the northern Dobunnic capital near Cirencester. This would hardly suggest a complete conquest, rather more a client relationship, with Bodvoc, as Professor Cunliffe suggests, as a puppet ruler.[36] The excavations at Bagendon, small-scale as they were, produced an astonishing amount of material, including some pre-conquest Roman imported pottery, thought at the time to be Arretine and similar to wares found at Camulodunum. This led to the idea of a strong trade relationship with the Catuvellauni.[37] Some doubt has, however, now been thrown on this by a re-examination of the pottery by G.B. Dannell who tells me that the 'Arretine' vase was made at Lezoux in Central Gaul and is quite different from the 'similar' wares found at Camulodunum.[38] It would seem from this that the Dobunni had their own supply route, either through Poole Harbour, or up the Severn. What is now required is a close examination of the pottery from other sites. From this a trade pattern will no doubt eventually emerge which may help to illuminate the political scene.

The one certain fact out of all this is the appearance of Verica as a suppliant before Claudius,[39] claiming that he had been driven out of Britain by an uprising and calling upon the Emperor to fulfil his obligations under their treaty. This offered the Romans a cast-iron justification for an invasion. But there is, of course, far more to it than this simple political expedient. The critical landing areas on the south-eastern coasts of Britain were now under hostile control, the political balance which had been so skilfully developed and maintained by Augustus had been totally wrecked. How, one might ask, could this happen after so much Roman influence and trade, spanning almost a century, had penetrated the south-east? The answer must be that there existed in Britain throughout this period a strong anti-Roman force which had been obliged to bow before the power and political realism of Cunobelinus, but found ready ears and hearts in the young princes, especially Caratacus. Such a force implies an organisation to ensure continuity and direction, and the obvious candidate is the Druidic priesthood. This religious hierachy was recruited from the ranks of the tribal nobility in the ancient priest/king tradition. No doubt Caratacus and Togodumnus had been initiated into the secret rites, and won over totally to the cause. All awaited the moment when the old king was too weak to rule or died. The political upset may not have come all at once, but by stages, starting with the removal of Adminius, the one son Cunobelinus felt he could trust with a strategically important area to rule. But soon Caratacus was in action, and we know from his subsequent career what a brilliant commander he was. The very small number of his coins show that his reign must have been very short: he had, after all, only two or three seasons before the Roman army was crossing the channel, the flight of Verica must have been in AD 40 or 41, to give time for Claudius to make his decision and plan his campaign.

4

The Conquest of AD 43

THE CAMPAIGN OF AULUS PLAUTIUS

The initial conquest of Britain had been carefully planned, executed and effectively completed within two years of landing. The Romans must have been very satisfied with the addition of a valuable province with such little effort and loss of life. If, however, any complacency existed in AD 45, it was soon to be rudely shattered by the British resistance movement, led at first by Caratacus, which was to make the Roman government wonder seriously if Britain was worth holding. The Roman leaders did not know that they faced 150 years of ferocious warfare and that Britain could not be considered to be a country of political stability until the third century. Claudius and his advisors were in a state of happy ignorance, and their conduct of self-congratulatory euphoria is easily understandable.

In this story only an outline of the events of these early years can be given,[1] but it must be seen in retrospect, since the seeds of the tragic events of AD 60 were being unwittingly dropped into fertile soil in the years which followed the landing of AD 43. Roman diplomacy had been successful since serious resistance collapsed after the one and only major battle, that of the Medway. One can judge where the Romans found and used their friends from the rewards which were duly given. There were two chief recipients – Prasutagus, of the Iceni, and Tiberius Claudius Cogidubnus, of the Regni and the Atrebates. But it does not necessarily follow that these men were rulers in Britain before AD 43. They were both given client kingdoms to rule with some degree of independence. Such arrangements were normal on the borders of the Empire where pro-Roman sympathies could be used to set up buffer zones to protect Roman territory against hostile peoples from without. This is how Rome used that powerful and wily woman Cartimandua, making her the Queen of the Brigantes to shelter the new province from trouble from the North. To have client kingdoms within a new province was an unusual decision, but rather typical of Claudius, who was shrewd enough to appreciate the need to acknowledge the importance of provincial leadership – a policy much disliked by the patricians of Rome.

These treaties were always made with individuals and there would never have been in the mind of the Emperor the idea that it would continue with the succession. It was to achieve a short-term aim, that of the rapid conquest and consolidation of Roman power in the lowlands. Exactly how these two men assisted the Roman army is not known, but it can be assumed that part of their help was through diplomatic pressure on wavering tribal rulers in central and south-western areas.

Cogidubnus was unable to persuade the Durotriges and the Belgae from resistance, but the rapidity of the Roman advance must owe much to his advice about the harbours along the south coast. The first of these was Bosham harbour in his own territory. (The evidence of this came from the excavations at Fishbourne with the discovery of a military store base under the later palace.) Cogidubnus worked closely with the legionary commander of the IInd *Augusta*, Titus Flavius Vespasian, who when he became emperor in AD 69 heaped further honours on him, including the exceptional status of an Imperial Legate. (This information comes from an inscription in Chichester.)[2] Claudius was anxious to extend the Roman franchise to provincials and most of the tribal leaders who had embraced the Roman cause would undoubtedly have become citizens, as did Cogidubnus, taking as his other two names those of his benefactor, Tiberius Claudius.

Although the Roman invasion was, under Aulus Plautius, well planned, the execution was fumbled at the start: at the last minute the troops refused to embark. This delay may have given the Britons cause to think that the whole project had been abandoned, as in the days of Gaius. They made no attempt to defend the coast, but pinned all their hopes on the crossing of the Medway. This was a hard two-day battle, which was won by an out-flanking movement by Batavian auxiliaries, who were trained to swim rivers in full armour. Once they had secured a footing on the west bank, the legionaries were ferried across, and, as soon as they were strong enough, the victory was theirs. In this decisive battle, the Britons were led by two brothers, Caratacus and Togodumnus, with their tribal levies. The account of this initial phase and the vital confrontation has survived only in Dio, and it is all too brief and somewhat garbled; but one useful piece of information about the Britons is included. This concerns the Dobunni, who had evidently been pressed into service, but promptly surrendered to Plautius before the fighting began. This may have been the result of diplomatic pressure exerted by Cogidubnus, as may also have been the rapid capitulation of the other tribes when Claudius himself arrived to lead his victorious troops into the British capital at Camulodunum. The inscription from his triumphal arch in Rome[3] records the submission of eleven British kings; one might make a shrewd guess at the identity of five or six,[4] but for the rest it would be useless speculation. The same statement seems to indicate that the Romans regarded the victory over the Ocean as the most praiseworthy, and that Britain was overcome with little bloodshed – a deft propa-

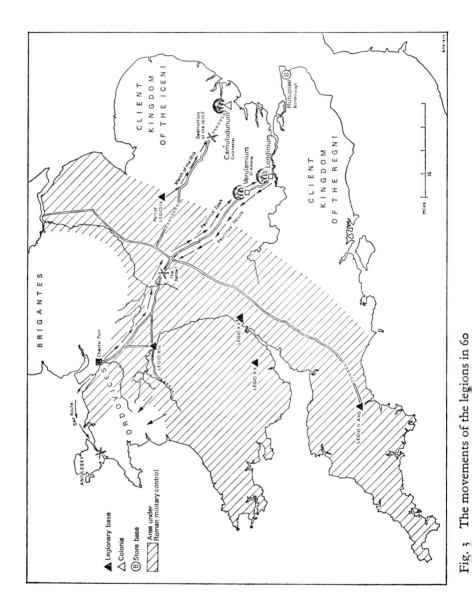

Fig. 3   The movements of the legions in 60

ganda touch to deceive the masses in Rome and enhance the standing of the Emperor.

We know little about the dispositions of the troops at this stage, except that Colchester became the main base with *Legio* XX in residence. There were probably forces at the other main British centres, even the friendly ones like Silchester, Cirencester and Verulamium. The only known hostility came from the south-west, where Vespasian had to deal with two warlike tribes. These must have been the Durotriges of Dorset and the Belgae of Hampshire and Wiltshire. There is dramatic evidence of this from Maiden Castle near Dorchester, from the excavations of 1934, directed by Sir Mortimer Wheeler. Aulus Plautius was well satisfied with his endeavours : a new province for Rome, south-east of a line from the Humber to the Bristol Channel, and as far to the west as the Exe, all taken with speed and efficiency and comparatively little loss (even if more than Rome was prepared to admit).

THE RAIDS OF CARATACUS

All this was dramatically changed by Caratacus at the end of the first governor's four-year term. The British prince saw how rapidly the anti-Roman resistance had collapsed and how the British rulers flocked to do homage to Claudius; there was no hope of continuing hostility in the South-East. He had to find peoples to lead who were tougher and who valued their freedom more highly. So he journeyed to the hill country to the west, beyond the Severn, taking with him no doubt like-minded Britons. There was no kinship between the tribes of these regions and those of the South-East; they had different ethnic origins, yet Caratacus was able to win over the important tribe of the Silures, who lived in the valley of the Usk and the Black Mountains, and direct them on a course of such implacable hatred of Rome that was to cost the new conquerors dear. How did Caratacus gain entry to these lands and their people, so remote from his own, and how did he win their support so rapidly? Accepting that he was a great personality, and carrying a challenging message, it is difficult to see how he could have achieved such remarkable success unaided. Roman diplomacy could hardly have been idle, but the smooth-tongued message that there was nothing to fear from Rome was rejected. Was Caratacus planning a conquest of the rich lowlands east of the Severn? Was this the dream of the hill folk penned in their territory by the thick fence of hill-forts along the marches?

Who knows? But one powerful element was to emerge later, which could have been effective at this time : the Druids had been forced to flee from their sanctuaries. They represented a religious force uniting all the Celtic peoples and they may well have been the means by which Caratacus was so quickly established as war-leader over peoples so far removed from his own kind. By the winter of 47–48, he was ready to strike and lead his warriors across the Lower Severn into the Province, or as Tacitus says 'into the territory of our allies'.[5] The moment was well chosen: Plautius had left to receive his ovation in Rome and the new governor was yet to arrive. No one expected war in the close season, and the Roman army was bedded down in its winter cantonments.

THE CAMPAIGN AGAINST CARATACUS

The careful planning, the swiftness and the violence of the attack alarmed Publius Ostorius Scapula, the incoming governor. He must have realised at the outset that he faced a powerful and determined enemy. The steps he took and the campaigns he instigated are given in a crisp outline by Tacitus; but he leaves out much vital detail which can only be supplied by a careful appraisal of the problems, both of the terrain and the aims of the two contenders.

The first step taken by Scapula was to clear the Province of the Britons on the rampage in the west. They had now split into bands, looking for loot and vengeance. There was therefore no question of a pitched battle: it was a matter of ordering the cavalry out to chase away 'the Indians'. Scapula realised the prime need was to seek and destroy the British leader and his forces, but the dispositions of the Roman units did not make this easy, since their frontier in the middle sector was far from the Severn and allowed Caratacus a good deal of room for manoeuvre. So he had to move his army forward, up to the Severn and then strike beyond to engage the Britons. The question he now asked himself was: could he safely strip the new province of the bulk of his troops? His answer illustrates his impetuous nature, which was to destroy at a stroke much of the careful diplomacy the Romans and their allies had developed over the previous years.

He needed a legion to block the lower Severn at the first crossing point above the estuary, where Gloucester now stands; his only spare major unit was *Legio* XX at Camulodunum, so a replacement there by veterans seemed logical and sensible. This was a sound and well-tried Roman practice, for the establishment of a *colonia* in newly conquered lands had several advantages. It was a useful way of pensioning off old soldiers by giving them grants of land; the city itself was laid out as a model to show the 'barbarians' what urban civilisation really meant; and it provided a reserve corps of battle-hardened troops which could be used in an emergency. Furthermore, it was usual for a commander to prepare his army for a difficult campaign by discharging the old and unfit, and filling their ranks with new recruits. At this period there was no set time for retirement. Although the soldiers were supposed to serve sixteen years, it was common for this regulation to be overlooked: it was a constant theme of complaint that legionaries were kept on until they were old and toothless. (The matter was only regularised under Vespasian who, an old soldier himself, brought in useful reforms.)

Scapula therefore unloaded his aged veterans and gave them the lands appropriated from the large royal estates of the Royal House. But what seems to have been a sensible step at the time was to develop into local unpleasantness. The rough soldiers, who were given a model town to live in, did not prove model citizens. Scapula may have been ignorant of, or chose to ignore, the aspirations of the Trinovantes, who had vainly imagined that the Romans were on their side. After all, it had been Caesar who had protected them against their formidable neighbours; they may too have had ideas about the return of their lands which were now being handed over to Roman soldiers, whose memories of the battle of the Medway would not have made them very friendly towards the Britons, and who could hardly be expected to distinguish one tribe from another.

Another decision of Scapula was to have even more serious repercussions. In a famous, much disputed, passage of Tacitus – *detrahere arma suspectis cunctaque cis Trisantonam et Sabrinam fluvios cohibere parat* – 'he disarmed those suspect in the areas on this [i.e. the Roman] side of the rivers Trent and Severn.' No one within the Province was by Roman law allowed to carry arms, excepting hunting weapons, unless he had a right to do so, and arms would have presumably been surrendered at the time of defeat or submission. The iron swords could have been quickly made by the skilled Celtic blacksmiths, so Scapula was clearly determined to intimidate the Britons and to prevent them from taking advantage of the withdrawal of Roman units. To make this effective, rigorous searches had to be carried out for arms in hidden places, and the owners of any that were found had to be punished. One can imagine the soldiers pulling down haystacks, rummaging in the native huts, emptying grain pits and knocking down anyone who got in their way. If this was the Governor's intention, it could not have found a better way of arousing bitter anti-Roman feelings. Nor was this activity confined to tribes who had been hostile or lukewarm towards Rome, but included, astonishingly enough, even the client kingdoms. This is apparent from a British reaction, for the first tribe to rebel against such treatment was the Iceni, who sought help from neighbouring tribes, the Coritani and the Catuvellauni on their borders. They must have attacked the soldiers sent on the hunt for arms and were then forced to defend themselves on a strong position. The description of Tacitus, of 'an enclosure surrounded by a crude and rustic kind of bank with a narrow entrance', could apply to a typical Iron Age hillfort seen through the Roman eyes. The revolt had to be put down quickly, so as not to interfere with the preparations for the campaign against Caratacus. Tacitus tells us that legionaries were not available, so auxiliaries were sent in – even though this meant using a dismounted cavalry unit. The incident was evidently considered small enough to be dealt with by a force of auxiliaries, which included a *cohors equitata.*

It would be interesting if the location of this local revolt could be resolved, but the evidence is not sufficient. Since Prasutagus kept his position of client king, it can be assumed that only a peripheral section of the tribe was involved, but that they were able to get help from beyond their borders. If this reasoning is correct, it limits the choice of place to the western or south-western areas of the tribe, but there are no known hillforts along this boundary which edges the Fens (at that period undrained) except Wandle-bury, near Cambridge. But this is probably too far to the south to have been Icenian territory, unless it was an outpost on the chalk ridge which is the only approach to the tribe's domain from that direction. It is, however, equidistant from the two known legionary bases at Camulodunum and Longthorpe. The nearest Roman unit was probably at Cambridge and that would have been very near unless it had already been moved to the west. The excavations at Wandlebury in 1955–6 did not produce any evidence which could have a bearing on the problem, so this episode must, for the present, remain without a reference point.

The incident may seem too trivial to merit serious attention, but its significance is that it reveals the quick reaction to the terror tactics of Scapula. They were effective in the short term and enabled him to muster his forces against the Britons in the west without fear of reprisals on his rear. But he left a mighty heap of smouldering embers, which needed only another fierce breath to bring them to a blaze. Scapula did not live to see the dire effects of the sacrifice of political considerations to military necessity – an action typical of generals at all times and in all places.

The campaign against Caratacus can be briefly summarised. The short crisp sentences of Tacitus give the order of events: first a punitive raid against the peoples of what is now north-west Wales, and the tribe named is the Deceangli of Flintshire. The purpose of this was the need for a geographical reconnaissance into territory unknown to Rome, to stop any native aid to the enemy. A warning shot was also needed across the bows of any Brigantian element which might have thought of bringing help to Caratacus. It had the effect of stirring some of the Brigantes into trouble, but the form it took is not clear from Tacitus, who refers to it as *discordiae* – a word he uses elsewhere[6] as an internal feud. Perhaps it means no more than a revolt against the client queen, Cartimandua. No Roman troops appear to be involved and the incident was settled by a few executions and pardons for the rest. But it illustrates the presence of a strong anti-Roman action in this frontier kingdom which was to gain strength at a later date.

Caratacus planted his standard in central Wales, choosing a defensive position with great care. He forced the legions into a frontal attack up a steep slope. After they had taken the stronghold, the Roman cavalry were unable to operate freely, owing to the thickly wooded terrain. Thus Scapula won a battle, but the war continued unabated, with the Silures all the more determined after they had heard that the Governor had unwisely sworn to exterminate the whole tribe.

The months that followed the defeat of Caratacus in the summer of 52 were perhaps the most crucial of all for Rome. Tacitus gives full rein to his descriptive talents for the battle itself – the capture of the British prince and his appearance in Rome (a piece of dramatic irony he could not fail to exploit); but the aftermath is briefly dismissed as if of little consequence. Yet from his fragmented comments it is possible to glean pieces of evidence which indicate a serious state of affairs for Rome. First a legionary detachment of 'some cohorts' under a camp prefect is attacked while building forts in Silurian territory. This would have consisted of at least a thousand men of *Legio* XX, and they were almost annihilated. A messenger got through to nearby forts and the cavalry dispersed the Britons, but the commander and eight centurions were lost – a large number for a detachment, unless it had consisted of three or four cohorts. This episode clearly illustrated the strength of the Silures in engaging a large legionary contingent and almost wiping it out, but it does not necessarily mean that these men were building a legionary fortress. Tacitus specifically states *extruendis . . . praesidiis* in the plural, so that detachments were building auxiliary forts and were, therefore, scattered at intervals of eight to ten miles over the region. Some of these building parties must have been overwhelmed while others hung on until help arrived, which helps to explain the heavy losses.

But the worst was to follow. A foraging party and cavalry sent to its aid were routed, further auxiliary units failed to stabilise the position and legions (which signifies at least two) were moved in before the enemy retired with only slight losses at the close of the day. This must be a much-shortened account of a serious campaign, since auxiliaries and legionaries were never close enough to be within a day's march of any given position; it certainly meant that the Silures were now operating in strength, using their terrain to advantage and were in a highly confident mood. There were several more engagements in this guerrilla warfare, including the two auxiliary cohorts which, according to Tacitus, were *intercepere* – a word with a stronger meaning than mere 'interception', but which softens the effect of destruction that is implied. There is a hint too that by now other tribes were involved and it is at this point that Scapula dies, a broken man. He may have been unwell on taking up his appointment, which would explain his choleric behaviour that intensified with the bitter frustration at the mounting tide of hostility, and at the inability of the Roman army to contain it. The vacancy was not expected in Rome and a new Governor had to be found quickly. But this took time, and the Silures, with renewed determination and overjoyed at the sudden death of their avowed enemy, extended their sphere of operations with increasing strength. They succeeded in defeating a legion in the field commanded by Manlius Valens, who was later to pay dearly for this in a slowing down of his career.

The success of the Britons affected events in the anti-Roman faction in the North and encouraged Venutius, the consort of Cartimandua, to declare himself its leader. This is a long and involved story, and at this stage the wily queen managed to retain control over her kingdom. Eventually, the third governor of Britain, A. Didius Gallus, arrived to take command late in 52. He was by now somewhat elderly, having been consul in 36 and having taken part in the invasion of Britain in command of the cavalry. After a lengthy and not undistinguished career, gossip in Rome implied that he badgered Claudius for another province. Since he may well have been one of the few qualified men who were immediately available, he was promptly given the task. Tacitus dismisses his governorship with contempt. Gallus was, he writes, 'heavy in years and many honours, and left matters to his subordinates with instructions to keep the enemy at a distance'. But during his long stay of six years in Britain, we hear of no further trouble. Had there been any more serious setbacks for Rome, Tacitus would surely have been able to dwell on the folly of sending such an old and inept governor at a time of crisis. One can but assume that the experienced Gallus must have crushed the Silures and, by effective defence measures, reduced them to a state of immobility. We have no means of knowing how this was done, but one can guess at a strong network of forts with tight communications west of the Severn, and excavations will eventually produce the evidence. The difficulty is that the kind of material for dating found in excavations cannot be precisely allocated to such a narrow period limit as to distinguish between, say, AD 52, 55 and 60; one needs coins in mint condition and large pottery assemblages for this.

There are more important conclusions to be drawn from the events of 48–54, both from the Roman and the British points of view. Claudius and his advisers must by now have been having second thoughts about Britain: the ease of the initial phases of the conquest had been dramatically succeeded by a wave of savage reaction from beyond the Severn, with heavy Roman losses. Although by 54 this frontier was tightly controlled these tribes remained free to continue their guerrilla tactics. There were rumblings from the North (though this may have seemed only an internal or family quarrel), but Roman units (including a legion) had already been engaged. It must therefore have been clear to close observers that Rome had serious problems on both fronts.

In the Province itself all was not well, for it is obvious from subsequent events that many of the Britons were not yet prepared to accept the Roman way of life and bitterly resented the small army of bureaucrats who were busy collecting taxes in their casual and callous way. The new colonists at Camulodunum were not behaving as model citizens, examples of a noble urban community. Many of them, barbarians themselves when recruited and brutalised by the harsh Roman army discipline, were treating the natives with total contempt, and with an assumption that everything in Britain was theirs for the picking. How much of all this was made known to Claudius and his advisers is impossible to say, but no attempt was made to deal with the frontier problem in a positive way, by extending the areas of conquest. Neither were efforts made to consolidate the gains and turn Britain into a secure Romanised province. There was disappointment too over the mineral resources; it was very soon apparent that the silver-yielding ores were of poor value and extraction costs too high, nor had any gold or copper yet been located; the only metal in abundance was iron. This, and the British captives put on the slave market, were the only immediate assets, and the question must have been asked, what was the value of the conquest – especially by those like the Seneca who had invested heavily in the Province. But to the Emperor it had been a matter of personal glory and fulfilment and there could be no going back. In these last years of his life he lost the desire to make any major decisions. Thus Britain remained a problem, with only part of the island securely held, and a very difficult frontier for the army to contain.

For the Britons, the conquest had been a traumatic experience. Those who had been hostile were now dead, enslaved or seething in silent anguish; those who had welcomed Rome now faced the realities of power and a corrupt monetary system. Those few who had benefited had wealth to lose and were themselves soon in competition with the horde of avaricious traders and touts, which poured into the country in the wake of the army. To the Britons within the Province now suffering in so many ways from the rough edges of army bureaucracy and capitalism, the natives beyond the frontier must have been envied for their freedom to continue the struggle against the new conquerers and to live their lives in the traditional way, however humble or lowly. These hidden feelings were roused and given hope by the strength and success of the resistance movement started by Caratacus, and continued with such vigour by the Silures. There, beyond the frontier were Britons who refused to be trodden into the ground under the iron-studded boots of the enemy. While they were still there, the possibility of release from the new tyranny must have stirred many a heart. Forces could have been at work to foster this hope, displacing the old tribal enmities with a new unity of purpose. Did the Druids now begin to exert their political and mystic powers to ferment and organise the resistance movement over the whole of Britain?

THE DRUIDS

Druidism was the one uniting force in Celtic society in Britain and Gaul, and may have been the most important political factor in the great Revolt. Unfortunately, the subject has been given so much absurd myth-making from the eighteenth century onwards, that the study of the Druids has been discredited.[7] Any assessment of Druidism must be based on Roman and Greek accounts, but since they are clearly biased and exaggerated, it is not easy to separate the reality from the early inventions and those of more recent times.

The power exerted by the Druidic priesthood stemmed from several elements. Firstly, they formed a special class in Celtic society, recruited from the landowning nobility immediately below the ruling tribal families; they were thus men of authority by birth and upbringing. But membership of the priesthood was not peculiar to individual tribes and the Druids were free to travel from one tribe to another, protected by their religious status. This is why the Druids, who operated from sanctuaries in south-eastern Britain, could move west and establish themselves in another sacred place in Anglesey and exercise their power over the tribes occupying Wales. Secondly, they were the preservers of tribal history and lore through the bards who committed all this to memory; but above all, they held the secrets of the gods and the power of magic. In primitive society throughout the world, the most important and feared people are the priests and medicine men, who are thought to be able to tap the mysteries of the unseen world and use them for – or against – both the tribe and its individual members who stray from the established rules.

But their position was much more complicated than this, for any priesthood held knowledge necessary for communities dependent on the land and on the seasonal changes. In Egypt, for example, the priest had by observation and deduction worked out the seasonal behaviour of the River Nile, which brings its rich silt laden flood waters every spring to revitalise the lands along its edges. Because the priests could foretell this annual event from their knowledge of the calendar, the people were led to believe that they actually created this phenomenon, such was the power and magic of knowledge. The priests knew the names of the gods, and could therefore call on them for help. They knew all the rites and rituals needed to pacify angry and vengeful deities. They thus stood between the people and the great unseen powers which could spread such fearful death and destruction in an instant. It was the terror created in primitive people by thunderstorms, earthquakes, eclipses and other natural events that was exploited by the priesthood to its advantage. As societies became more sophisticated, they began to keep records of the movements of heavenly bodies and of tribute due to them and this led to the development of writing. In the Middle Ages in Britain, the clerk and the priest were synonymous: a person brought to court and found guilty could ask for a book and, if he read from it, would automatically be considered to have 'benefit of clergy', and therefore, not subject to civil law; this practice was not wholly repealed until 1827.

The Druids certainly had knowledge of the movements of the stars and planets and were able to construct a calendar, according to Pliny, by the lunar observations; but such detailed knowledge goes back much earlier in Britain, if we are to believe some of the recent mathematical studies of the

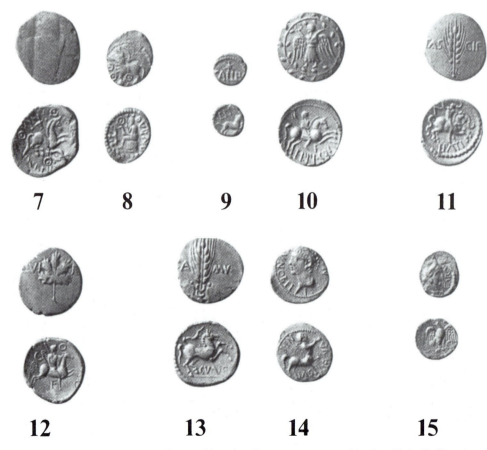

1   *Previous page*   Boudica and her daughters, as portrayed in the Civic Hall, Cardiff

2   Coins of British rulers. 1 Commius 2 Tincommius 3–4 Tasciovanus 5–6 Addedomaros 7–8 Dubnovellaunus (Kent/Essex) 9–10 Eppilus (Atrebates/Kent) 11 Epaticcus 12 Verica 13–14 Cunobelinus 15 Caratacus

3 Head-hunting: a scene from Trajan's Column. Two Celtic auxiliaries are offering enemy heads to the Emperor Trajan; auxiliary infantry stand on his left.

4 The Roman army building
camps with turf ramparts,
timber towers, gates and
a bridge: from Trajan's
Column

5 *opposite* The Emperor
Nero: bronze statuette,
found at Baylham House,
Suffolk. It is decorated
with silver and neillo inlay

6 The Emperor
Claudius: bronze head,
found in the River
Alde

7 *top* The fort at Ixworth in East Anglia: air photograph, by Professor J. K. St Joseph. The triple ditches are shown as differences in crop growth, and there are indications of internal timber buildings

8   Crop-marks of a marching camp at Horstead-with-Stanninghall, Norfolk

9 *top* Crop-marks, including a marching camp with its well-rounded corner, near Stuston, Suffolk

10 *top* The gyrus at The Lunt, near Coventry: a reconstructed view by Alan Sorrell

11   The granary at The Lunt: a reconstruction

12   The Lunt: reconstruction of the defences

13   Length of wattle-and-daub wall, baked hard in destruction of Colchester
AD 60

14 *top* Dates burnt in the Boudican destruction at Colchester

15 *opposite* The tombstone of Longinus from Colchester

16 *above* The Temple of Claudius at Colchester: a model

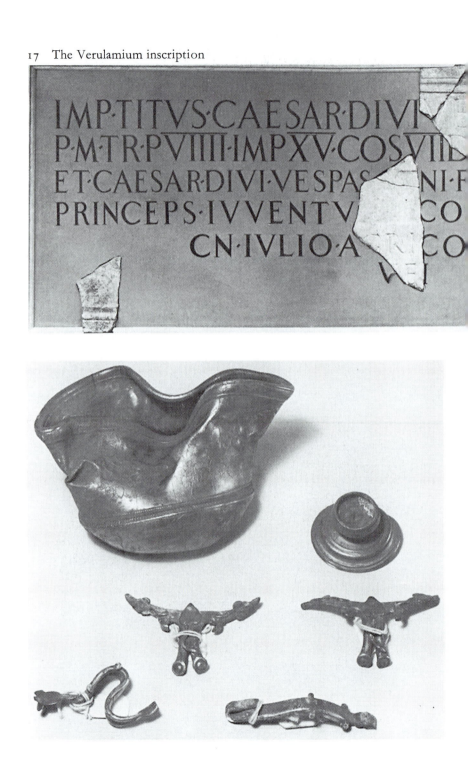

IMP·TITVS·CAESAR·DIVI
P·M·TR·P·VIIII·IMP·XV·COS·VII
ET·CAESAR·DIVI·VESPAS   NI·F
PRINCEPS·IVVENTV   CO
          CN·IVLIO·A   CO

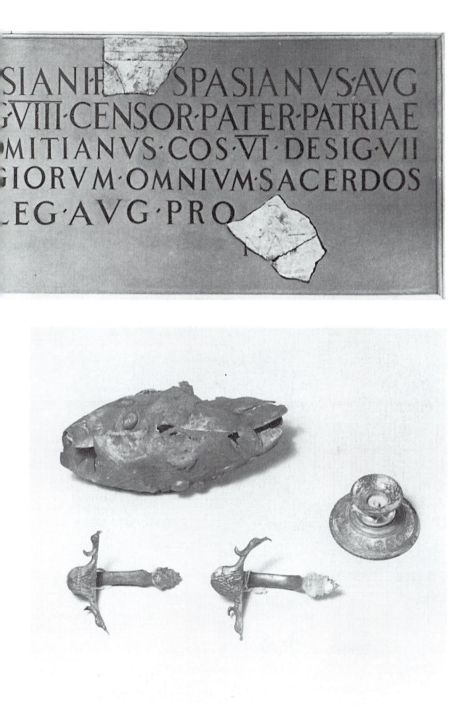

SIANI[ ]SPASIANVS·AVG
[ ]·VIII·CENSOR·PATER·PATRIAE
[ ]MITIANVS·COS·VI·DESIG·VII
[ ]GIORVM·OMNIVM·SACERDOS
[ ]·EG·AVG·PRO[ ]

18 and 19   The silver cups from Hockwold

20 Excavation of lower courses of a Roman bastion in the city wall at
London. The stone marked 'B' is a block from the tombstone of Classicianus

21 *top* Details of block B

22 Heap of masonry, including two stones from tombstone of Classicianus: an engraving of 1852

23 *top* The reconstructed tombstone of the Procurator Julius Classicianus

24 The Hawkedon gladiator's helmet

megaliths and stone circles. Contact with the Greek and Roman world introduced literacy, and the Druids were able to put some of their knowledge into epigraphic form, like the Coligny Calendar, a large engraved bronze plate found in fragments in 1897 in a vineyard in Gaul. This appears to be a table divided into 62 months (almost five years) with lucky and unlucky days indicated.[8]

There is little knowledge of the rituals practised by the Druids since they were kept highly secret, and classical writers wrote mainly on the basis of rumour and travellers' tales. This, of course, has led to the invention of some highly imaginative accounts, like that of Posidonius, of the great cage of wickerwork in which human beings were imprisoned and burnt as sacrifices. Many of the ideas about the Druids and the ancient Britons generally are derived from the seventeenth and eighteenth centuries, based on observations of the North American Indians. The concept of the 'noble savages' is that of a creature surviving in a kind of natural purity unaffected by the vices of sophisticated society – a theme popular with the puritanical writers of the period. The ancient Briton, in his skins and woad, is still an archetypal figure embedded in the minds of many, even today. More recent studies of primitive peoples, who were still to be found unaffected by contact with modern 'civilisation' in remote areas a hundred years ago, have shed a totally different light on the origins and development of human societies. Archaeology has produced evidence in quantity of sanctuaries and rituals, but these are difficult to understand, since the structures and objects in themselves often give little indication of their function.

There are some aspects of Celtic religion which are in no way connected with the Druids. Shrines and sanctuaries in Celtic Europe are common, and belong to local deities associated with hills, streams, springs and natural places, or were peculiar to tribal groups. Many names of these deities have survived on altars of Roman times: there are statues and reliefs on some of them. It is clear from this that the religious belief of the Celts was basically animistic, that is to say they created personalities for members of the great unseen spirit world. The Druids operated at a higher level, since they had an understanding of the Universe, and were capable of developing subtle philosophical ideas out of it. There are two Celtic practices which are widespread and with which the Druids may have been connected – the reverence for the human head and the votive deposit as a sacrifice to the gods. The human head, or *tête coupée*, appears commonly in statuary and reliefs and clearly had an important place in Celtic beliefs.[9] It was thought that the head was the centre of the soul, and contained the very essence of the man – not an unreasonable assumption since it contains a concentration of the major senses. This idea led to the practice of head hunting, depicted on Trajan's Column, where Celtic auxiliaries are seen offering the Emperor enemy heads taken in a skirmish (3). Heads of those vanquished in battle were highly prized and kept as family heirlooms, or were offered to the

E

gods. It was thought that physical qualities such as courage and strength could in this way be passed on to the victor. All over the Celtic world, especially in Gaul, there are reliefs showing heads, and in Britain many examples of stone heads have been found, but rarely is it possible to date them. It is a motif often found as a decorative mount, as on the famous Aylesford bucket.[10]

If more shrines and sanctuaries could be found and carefully excavated, evidence might be recovered of cult practices, possibly associated with the reverence of the human head. There are many religious sites of the period in Britain, but in most cases one suspects that the Celtic structures were superseded by the large and more massive stonework of Roman times. The Romans always showed a healthy respect for the deities and spirits of strange countries, since they believed that these resident powers could operate against them unless they were identified and placated. This is why all the places sacred in Britain were likely to be venerated and became centres of ritual. Unfortunately, investigations in the past on the sites of Romano-British temples have not always recognised this important aspect, and attention has been directed only on the later remains. There are occasional examples of Celtic temples for which there was no continuity. One of these was found in a wartime excavation by Professor W. F. Grimes, on the site of the London airport at Heathrow.[11] It was a timber shrine of a rectangular plan with a colonnade on all four sides. The evidence of the pottery showed that it had had a long life and had been renewed several times: there was even a suggestion that an attempt had been made to continue its function after the Conquest, but this was never completed. On the north side were eleven huts of a small community living by the sacred place.

One of the more remarkable types of structure is the so-called ritual shaft, which has the appearance of a well, but the filling clearly indicates another purpose. Objects are often found which have been carefully placed in the shaft. The strangest, perhaps, is the trunk of a cypress tree in Gaul, while one in Germany had a wooden stake set in the bottom, with remains about it which have been interpreted as human, suggesting a sacrifice. Almost of all contain 'votive' objects – pottery, bronze cauldrons, carved wood statuettes and other objects which can be seen as offerings to the gods. In many cases, too, the objects have been deliberately broken or 'killed', as in human sacrifices. These shafts may have been dug in an effort to approach the deities of the underworld. Votive deposits are by no means confined to these strange shafts, but are also common in lakes, pools and even marshy places, as seen in the series of human sacrifices in the peat bogs of Denmark. Hoards of metalwork have been found in such places, and have obviously been deliberately thrown in to appease the gods, in many cases broken or 'sacrificed' beforehand. The discovery of such hoards in lakes and rivers and wells is commonplace, and, as one would expect, the practice continues into Roman times. The most remarkable well deposit is that from

Coventina's Well on Hadrian's Wall. Even today people are still anxious to throw their small change into wells and fountains, hoping for their dreams and desires to come true. So this ritual never dies.

The most important of these hoards, which could have a direct relationship to the revolt of 60, is that from Llyn Cerrig Bach in Anglesey. This was a wartime discovery in 1943, and published with commendable promptitude by Sir Cyril Fox in 1946.[12] Peat was required to be spread over the surface of the RAF station at Valley, and dug up mechanically from a nearby lake for this purpose. The workmen noticed pieces of ironwork in the peat, in particular a length of chain which was used by a tractor for pulling a lorry out of a soft place. Eventually, word was passed to the National Museum of Wales and immediately every effort was made to collect together all the bits and pieces scattered over the airfield. They added up to an impressive total of 138, mostly of iron, but there were some of bronze and wood. Doubtless it represents only a portion of objects dragged out of the lake, and much more must still be there. One complete iron wheel tyre was actually thrown back when the peat was being hauled out by a scoop on a cable. The careful study by Sir Cyril Fox led to the conclusion that the material was predominantly military – swords, spears, chariot fittings and harness; that it could not be later than the middle of the first century AD and that the hoard included objects from different parts of Britain, but mainly from the south-west. He regarded it as a part of a votive deposit of tribute gathered from many parts of Britain. In view of the importance of Anglesey as the target of the Roman campaign of AD 59–60, the deposit must have been associated with the Druids.

THE ACCESSION OF NERO AND THE ADVANCE INTO WALES

A decisive event for Britain was the assassination of Claudius in October of AD 54 and the immediate assumption of power by the youthful Nero at the age of seventeen. In the final years of his reign, Claudius had displayed a woeful inactivity and lack of decision, which caused a maintenance of the *status quo*. Nowhere is that better illustrated than in Britain, where Didius Gallus was, with some difficulty, holding frontiers by then outdated by circumstances. In his early years as emperor, Nero was much under the influence of his two trusted advisors, Seneca and Burrus, and of Agrippina, his ambitious mother. It is evident from the prompt intervention in Armenia that there was a new decisiveness at the centre: Corbulo was despatched in 55 to settle by force the difficult frontier problems with the Parthians. The British situation may not have seemed so urgent, but Didius Gallus had served his normal term (which for a governor was three to four years), and it is difficult to understand why he was not replaced in 55–56. One of the men now in control, Seneca, had, according to Dio, a vested interest in Britain, having lent some of the chiefs the vast sum of forty million *sesterces* at a high rate of interest. His sudden withdrawal of this money is given as one of the causes of the Revolt. It may be an exaggerated and garbled version of an incident used by Dio, to blacken the character of Seneca; the historian shows an antipathy towards philosophers and like many of his contemporaries chose to spice his pages with gossip. There is a possibility that the loans were made by Claudius and were being called in by Seneca on behalf of Nero. Tacitus is silent on this point, but for any connection between this story and the Revolt, it must have taken place within two or three years prior to 60.

The time when the most obvious concern was felt about the future of Britain was immediately after the death of Scapula in 52, and before Gallus had taken control. There is a sentence in the life of Nero by Suetonius Tranquillus, which may have a bearing on this matter: 'Nero', he wrote, 'considered a withdrawal from Britain, yet kept his forces there since such a situation would have reflected adversely on the glory gained by Claudius.' Some historians assume that this decision was made after the Revolt, but by 60–61 Nero no longer had these pious thoughts towards his adoptive father, and, in any case, it would have meant the admission of a great defeat. The possibility of a withdrawal would fit more readily into the early years of Nero's reign. This brings us back to Seneca. Something may have caused him to review his own, or the Emperor's financial stake in Britain. This could have been a discussion about the value of the Province and whether it would not have been better to pull out when it could have been done without a loss of face, rather than suffer further heavy losses. If such arguments were being advanced in the inner court circle in Rome, they could have only been the result of gloomy reports of the situation sent in by the Governor, and Seneca may have been worried enough to have withdrawn his, or the imperial, loans all at once, regardless of the consequences. But, as we have only Dio's evidence, the whole argument must remain speculative.

There was undoubtedly a case for serious concern over the future of Britain in Rome during the years 54 to 56, and a decision was now required. This came in 57 and it was for positive action on the western frontier: the whole of the area we now know as Wales was to be conquered and held. Whether this was a realistic assessment of the British position, we will never know, nor can we appreciate the factors which decided the issue. It could be that it was only at this time that the Romans discovered that there was gold in central Wales, silver in north Wales and copper in Anglesey. The defeat of the Deceangli had already brought the Roman presence into Flintshire and information about the unconquered areas could have been obtained. Add to this the rich iron deposits in the Forest of Dean – and the mineral prospects of Britain could have seemed bright enough. But to make this a key factor in the crucial decision would be pure guesswork.

The new man chosen for the forward movement was Quintus Veranius, who had been the first Governor of Lycia and Pamphylia, which was taken over as an Imperial province under Claudius in AD 43 to put an end to the savage vendettas pursued by the inhabitants. He was an important figure in Rome and one of the small group of senators sent to acknowledge Claudius after he had been acclaimed by the praetorians after the murder of Gaius. Veranius was known for his diplomacy and this is probably why Claudius gave him such a difficult assignment in Asia Minor. Part of an inscription giving his career was found near Rome in 1926.[13] This credits him with a victory over a hill tribe which would have given him experience in mountain warfare in difficult terrain. His reputation as a military man is confirmed by the Greek author Onasander, who dedicated to him a book on military science called *The General*. On his return to Rome in 49 he became consul and afterwards was raised to patrician status and made an augur. The inscription is tantalising and difficult to complete, but there is a likely suggestion that Veranius was appointed to Britain *cum non petierit*, ('without seeking the post'). If this is an accurate reading, it would seem to refer to Didius Gallus, who had pleaded so hard for a province.

The question arising from this is why it was felt necessary to send such a distinguished and experienced diplomat to Britain, on what would appear to be purely a military mission. It brings us back to Dio's story of the loans suddenly called in. If there had been a change of policy and the British chiefs were in a state of shock and humiliation, the choice of Veranius as governor can be understood; and his military record suited him also for the advance into Wales, where diplomacy could also have been an advantage in any attempt to isolate the Silures. Unfortunately, no answer to these problems is possible, since Veranius died within a year of arriving in Britain. Subsequent events show that, whatever efforts he may have directed towards the chiefs within the Province, they were of no avail. The more significant facts are that the Silures are never referred to again as a hostile force, and his successor was free to move against the Ordovices. Tacitus tells us that Veranius had at least one season against the Silures, but he dismisses it contemptuously as a few raids of no significance. It is highly unlikely that the Governor would have wasted his time in such a manner; indeed his own view of his task in Britain is revealed in his will, in which he stated that, if he had lived out his full term of three years in Britain, he would have completed the assignment. Tacitus here is at fault in slipping into an unpardonable aside in accusing Veranius of undue flattery to Nero, when clearly he was seeking to secure the safety of his family by diplomatic means. Tacitus is more concerned to prepare a platform from which to extol the great success of Paullinus, whom he is anxious to portray as a great man wronged by Nero, and this allows a political colouring in the *Annals* to distort the truth.

5

The Storm Breaks AD 60

Quintus Veranius probably came to Britain in the winter of 57–58 and died in the summer or autumn of 58. His appointment had been made by Nero's advisers with due care and consideration, and the experience and seniority of Veranius leave one in no doubt that there were difficult problems to be faced in Britain, since, whatever we think of the story of the loans, Seneca must have been aware of the groundswell of discontent in the Province. The vacancy left by the Governor's sudden death had to be filled quickly, since a considerable campaign had been mounted, and needed to be brought to a successful conclusion. In the search for a successor, military considerations were probably paramount, and there could not have been many men who were both available and suitably qualified. The choice fell on Caius Suetonius Paullinus, a hard, uncompromising soldier, totally lacking the skills and graces of a diplomat. We know little of his early career. He may have been consul in 42 or 43; before this he was sent to Mauretania to put down a serious revolt. He was the first Roman commander to cross the Atlas mountains and advance miles beyond; according to Pliny the Elder, it took him ten days to reach the summit. It may have been this experience of mountain warfare that was the deciding factor in his choice. He probably arrived in Britain late in 58 or early 59 and, according to Tacitus, had two successful seasons in 59 and 60 before disaster struck.

At some point during these years, the Romans came to realise that the centre of discontent and hostility towards them emanated from the sacred groves of the Druids in Anglesey, where those Britons had gathered who followed the lead of Caratacus in refusing to submit to Rome. It may even be that Veranius attempted to draw wavering British loyalties towards Rome, or at least to cast doubts on the efficacy of the priests. If so, he was soon left in no doubt that it was beyond his powers of persuasion. The only possible choice left open to Rome was the destruction of the Druidic power in Britain. This decision could only have been reached with great reluctance, since Rome always showed the utmost respect for local gods and native religious sympathies. They knew how dangerous it could be to interfere with the strong fears and beliefs of unsophisticated people; changes could be expected after years of assimilation with Rome, especially through service in the army, but this required generations of time. Here, however, was a stark and immediate reality. In the pre-Christian period of Imperial Rome, there were only two occasions when the State was forced to move against a nation's religion – in Britain and Judaea. In both cases the results were terrifying. It was only in Britain that success could be acclaimed; the Jews remain to this day totally – one could almost say fanatically – attached to their God.

One must assume that the reduction of Wales involved Anglesey from the start, and that it was necessary to defeat the Silures to avoid trouble on the flank of any advance to the north-west. As yet, we know little, from archaeology, of the details of the three seasons of campaigns; but when that of 60 opened, Paullinus was free to move directly towards Anglesey. The army was probably established at Chester on the Dee, where the winter was spent in preparing for a seaborne invasion and supply train with flat bottomed boats. Paullinus must also have secured the upper Severn, as far as, if not beyond, the key-point of Caersws, and have moved his troops into the territory of the Deceangli (of Flintshire), who had earlier been forced to submit to Scapula. Thus Snowdonia, and the area controlled by the Ordovices was tightly surrounded at the start of the season, and the Roman army was then poised for a sudden thrust by land and sea towards the sanctuaries of the Druids.

One must now take up the narrative from Tacitus, who clearly sets out the train of events in *Annals*, XIV. The Roman attack had reached its point of culmination on the Menai Straits, when Paullinus was informed of the Revolt, and the historian then sets out the causes. Prasutagus, king of the Iceni, had died and this ended the special client relationship of the tribe with Rome, which was, even for Claudius, an odd arrangement, made only, one presumes, in return for notable services rendered at the time of the invasion. By then, with the extension of the Province towards the West, it was an awkward anomaly unlikely to find any support for its continuity with the new rulers in Rome. In any event, the creation of a client ruler was entirely a personal matter and there could not have been any question of a consort succeeding. Boudica must surely have appreciated this situation although some of her lowly subjects may not. The King named the Emperor as his co-heir with his two daughters. He presumably had no son, and vainly imagined that such a will would have secured half the property for his family.

It appears that in the case of Herod, Augustus took the view that the personal fortune and estates of a client King became Imperial property on his death.[1] It is possible, therefore, that the Procurator of Britain at the time, Decianus Catus, operated entirely with Imperial approval, if not direct instruction, in ensuring that the whole estate of Prasutagus was taken over, and the only way this could have been achieved was by a full inventory of lands, livestock, family plate and jewels and all portable wealth. This would have been a fine opportunity for an unscrupulous man to fiddle the accounts to secure a fat percentage for himself. This was common practice among these financial officers, and the State did not intervene unless the proportion of taxes, or other dues so collected, was excessive. Verres, the infamous Praetor of Sicily, admitted that he needed to make three fortunes in his term of office, one to pay his way, one for bribes, and a third for his retirement – but this was in the free and easy days of the Republic. Decianus Catus was well within his rights in making a full inventory and considered himself and his staff free to help themselves to any juicy pickings. The junior officers and collectors were mostly old legionaries serving as *beneficiarii*. Although long past active service, the military bearing and training made them useful in the roles of police, toll and tax collectors, and they would not have been above a little looting or bribery; there were also the slaves of the Procurator, who acted as clerks and secretaries. These were the kind of men who appeared unheralded at the royal palace of the Iceni. Boudica naturally assumed that her status and regal bearing would have overawed the Roman officials, but they were merely annoyed at their actions being questioned.

To these Romans, the British were little more than barbarians recently brought to submission; the niceties of treaties and favoured clientship would hardly have bothered them. Resistance was treated as an act of rebellion and the infuriated Queen suffered the indignity of being stripped and lashed like a common criminal, and her daughters, as spoils of war, were raped by all and sundry. Property and possessions of all the chief tribal families were seized; the Emperor was entitled to half, but by this act of defiance the Iceni lost the remainder – at least it could be so interpreted by an unscrupulous procurator.

All this was but the match applied to a highly combustible situation. The deeper causes have already been mentioned, starting with the rash terror tactics of Scapula, then the setting up of the *colonia*, then the demand of the loans by Seneca; finally, according to Dio, the Procurator was doing the same on behalf of the Emperor. The Trinovantes were ready for an insurrection: they had suffered too much from the new colonists and the land appropriations. The veterans, says Tacitus, had been turning the natives out of the houses and lands. Even if this had been done legally with adequate compensation, there is little worse for a family than to be moved from lands by force – the same bitter feelings are common today in the face of compulsory purchases by government departments. Another serious grievance was the great temple of Claudius at Camulodunum, described as *arx aeternae dominationis*, a stronghold of eternal despotism.

As the temple was dedicated to the deified Claudius, it could not have been built before his death in AD 54, as Duncan Fishwick has pointed out.[2] The words used by Tacitus, *templum divo Claudio constitutum*, must mean that the building had not yet been consecrated, but only decreed by the Senate. Yet an edifice was standing in 60, since the veterans used its massive walls for their last stand. So it seems reasonable to suppose that it was under construction, and it is hardly surprising that such a large and ornate building should take over five years to complete. The implication of this is that, on the deification following the death of Claudius, the Senate decided that a temple should be dedicated to him in the place of his greatest and only triumph – Britain. It is also very likely that the area had already been made sacred by the erection of an altar, probably dedicated to Rome and the Imperial cult, at which the Council of Britain would pay their annual respects, as at the altar of the Three Gauls at Lugdunum. What the British chiefs objected to so strongly was not this modest service, but the contribution they were obliged to make to the building of the temple, which, if construction started in 55, would need to be financed from 56 onward. If this date is correct, this serious piece of aggravation is brought nearer to the date of the Revolt. For the Druids it offered a most timely opportunity for anti-Roman propaganda which they doubtless exploited to the full. The very thought of a great temple, not merely to an alien cult, but to the very man who had enslaved Britain, was enough, but, worse, the Britons were forced to pay for it. It came too at the moment when the Druids must have realised, as soon as the decision had been made to conquer Wales, that their sanctuary was no longer in a safe area. This view was strengthened when Veranius began to take stock of the situation in the winter of 56–57.

We thus have here three main causes of the Revolt: the appropriation of lands and brutal behaviour of the colonists towards the Trinovantes; the building of the temple; and, the final straw, the seizure of the royal properties of the Iceni, and the violence and shameful acts against Boudica and her daughters. But the background must not be forgotten. The act of conquest, humiliating to many Britons, the rash terror tactics of Scapula in 48, the continuing harassment by Roman officials and foreign traders, the money and loans transactions, which men not used to a capitalist economy did not fully understand. All these grievances were kept alive and fanned into hot resentment by the constant and insidious stream of propaganda from the Druids, in a desperate effort to save their sacred places.

THE UPRISING AND DESTRUCTION OF CAMULODUNUM

Such is part of the intricate pattern of political intrigue we can recreate from the scraps of evidence provided by Tacitus and Dio. Tacitus makes another interesting point – that the colony of Camulodunum was undefended. This is difficult to understand since it was laid out inside the defences of the abandoned legionary fortress, but archaeology has shown that these were levelled, and not kept in commission for the colonists. Both historians list signs and portents, necessary parts of the narrative to audiences who expected such phenomena at times of catastrophe. According to Tacitus, the statue of Victory, which would have been part of the provincial altar, fell face down as if in retreat. Women had hysterics, and shouts in foreign tongues were heard in the Senate House; there were howling noises in the theatre (*consonuisse ululatibus*); a vision had been seen reflected in the Thames of a devastated colony; the sea had the colour of blood and the ebb tide left heaps on the shore that looked like human bodies. One wonders how many stories like these were put around by the Britons to alarm the superstitious veterans.

As soon as the veterans realised that a Revolt had become a reality, they looked around for help. But the only troops available, apart from a small number in the colony, were 200 in London, consisting of a few soldiers for protecting property, messengers and officials seconded for civil duties but, although old for service, still on the army list, who were, says Tacitus, not fully equipped. The veterans were clearly taken by surprise and panicked, for they did not draw up their forces behind any defences, or send the women, children and elderly to places of safety. Any plans they devised in these terrifying hours were questioned by secret supporters of the Britons, planted in the colony. The kind of sabotage perpetrated, combined with a whispering campaign, suggests well-planned and executed tactics. The Britons swept all before them and overran the settlement at the first onslaught. The soldiers and veterans took refuge in the walls of the unfinished temple, and held out for two days, hoping all the time for a relief force, but it never reached the stricken city.

Paullinus had ordered the only available legion, the Ninth, to put down the Revolt, but the Roman units were spread out like a network. For it was not usual in Britain at this time to have complete legions in their fortresses; the headquarters and first cohort occupied forts of 20–25 acres, with other cohorts or auxiliary units. The commander of the Ninth was Petillius Cerealis, who was later to play an important role in the Civil War of 67 and became Governor of Britain in 71. His subsequent career shows him to have been a rash and impetuous soldier. Had he been more cautious, he would have collected together a reasonable force to deal with the insurgents. Instead of this he took the men he had, some 2000 legionaries and auxiliary cavalry, and rushed down to Colchester. He probably had the first cohort and possibly two others from the Ninth Legion, and a unit of 500 horsemen.

His hope of surprising the Britons and crushing the Revolt at an early stage misfired, since this possibility had been foreseen. The Romans, by forced marches of twenty-five miles a day, could have reached Camulodunum in three days – travelling almost due south to Durovigutum (Godmanchester), then along the main supply route direct to the *colonia* (a route later to be superseded when London became the nucleus of the road system).

There are enough pieces of this early road to be certain that this existed as the principal route connecting Camulodunum with the western frontier. Cerealis never reached the hard-pressed veterans to save them from destruction. At some point a force of Britons was waiting, presumably in a carefully planned ambush. His legionaries were cut to pieces, the General narrowly escaping by cutting a path through the surrounding horde with his cavalry and riding back to his base on the Nene. It is impossible to know when this happened or the precise timing relative to the Revolt. One could guess that it was twenty to thirty miles from Camulodunum in wooded country suitable for a surprise attack. From his subsequent career Cerealis emerges as a commander prepared to take undue risks and he was pressing hard to reach the colonists. It was no time for a cautious approach with advance scouting parties and a thorough search of the woods along the route. The British must have laid their plans well to have overcome such a strong force of tough legionaries. By attacking them while in extended line of march, the Britons gave the enemy little opportunity to move into battle formation. The Roman legionaries were thus cut into isolated groups. Doubtless they sold their lives dearly, and the Britons lost many of their best fighting men on that day.

Did Cerealis make the dash on his own initiative on hearing of the trouble, or did he wait for orders from Suetonius? The probability is that his responsibility was to protect the rearward areas while the bulk of the army was in a forward position. It may well therefore have been within his powers to have attempted to crush the Revolt as soon as he had information about it, at the same time informing the Governor of the situation and his plans to deal with it. In this case, it is possible that he could have reached the colonists before they succumbed, and this means that the Britons had divided their forces against this contingency.

There was time at least for the small force of 200 men to be sent from London. But there is no indication that any kind of defences were thrown together and none had been provided in the plans of the *colonia*. This may be seen as a surprising omission, but it also underlies the supreme confidence of the Romans. The archaeological evidence from the Lion Walk (see Chapter 7) shows that the turf bank of the legionary fortress had been levelled out and buildings erected over them. But even if these defences existed, it is doubtful whether there was a large enough force of old soldiers fit and able enough to man them, since the circuit of *c.* 1800 m. would have needed at least 1500 men with full equipment, and artillery at the corners and interval towers.

Their only hope was the thick walls of the great temple of the deified Claudius, still in a state of construction. Here the tough veterans might hope to hold out long enough for help to come. But it was such a small area that the Britons could concentrate all their efforts on to it by throwing continuous missiles and by heaping burning brushwood round the walls.

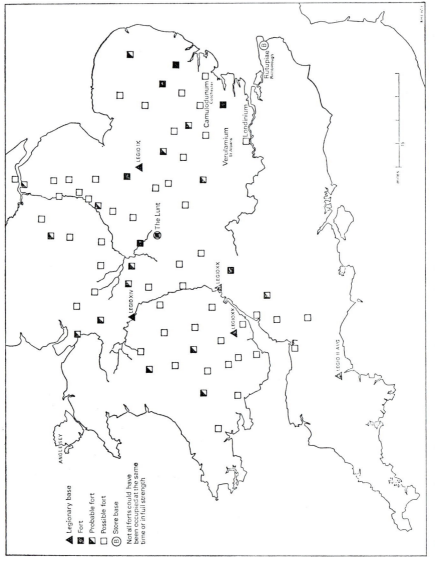

Fig. 4 Military dispositions under Suetonius Paullinus

Legionary base
Fort
Probable fort
Possible fort
B Store base

Not all forts could have
been occupied at the same
time or in full strength

ANGLESEY

LEGIO XIV

LEGIO IX

The Lunt

LEGIO XX

LEGIO XX

LEGIO II AVG

Camulodunum
Colchester

Verulamium
St Albans

Londinium

Rutupiae
Richborough

miles   15

The Romans were trapped, totally unable to keep the natives at a distance, as soon as their own supply of missiles was exhausted. The enclosure was packed with survivors, men, women and children, overcome by the great heat, fire, smoke and rain of spears which never stopped. In two days it was all over. The hated veterans and their equally reviled citadel, fell. The Britons had achieved a remarkable success – which immediately went to their heads.

THE SACK OF LONDON AND VERULAMIUM

Up to this point the Britons have achieved enormous successes – the destruction of the hated colony and its veterans, and of a strong legionary force. One feels also that there had been careful planning with a sense of anticipation and use of a kind of fifth column to spread alarm among the veterans. But, from this moment onward, the Romans took command and dictated the terms of the battle. This initiative must undoubtedly be attributed to Paulinus, who was now asserting his authority. But had the Britons lost their sense of tactical judgement? The elation of the victorious Britons at their astounding success created a sense of wild euphoria, which for the moment obliterated any appreciation of the immediate realities and the need for rapid action to forestall or anticipate Roman reaction. While most of the Britons were engrossed in their celebrations, others were more intent on searching for loot and fugitives, not merely in the *colonia*, but in the isolated farms and settlements. The task of bringing the rebels back to an organised force took time – time enough for the Governor to hurry back from Anglesey and take stock of the position.

Paullinus would have felt then the urgent need to see for himself the extent and state of the Revolt. The distance from Anglesey to London by road is about 250 miles, but he would have sailed by a fast galley, assisted by the westerly winds, to Chester and reduced his road journey to about 180 miles, which could have taken him three or four days of hard riding[3] with a detachment of cavalry. He would have alerted all the units he passed along the road and arranged for supplies for his army, which was following on foot at a steady twenty-miles-a-day slog. Tacitus tells us that he reached London before the Britons and was able to see the position for himself. Had the British forces been under a disciplined command, they would have already taken London and been waiting for him as they had for Cerealis. But the extent to which the Britons were now out of control is shown by the ability of Paullinus and his small force of cavalry to reach London and review the position.

He immediately saw that it was now a completely hopeless one for the inhabitants. The Procurator had already fled to Gaul to vanish from history. The richer traders and citizens followed in any craft they could pay for, seize or commandeer. The rest made a pathetic plea to the Governor to save them from the awful fate about to engulf them. But what could the

Governor do? There was no question of putting the place into a state of defence: it was a sprawling shanty town, the only large buildings being those of the Government offices, the warehouses by the river and a few houses of the wealthy traders. Those with good horses could join him on his return journey, if they could keep pace with the cavalry, or take a chance of travelling along Watling Street as quickly as possible into the safety of the military zone. Nor could he tell the people of his plans, lest they reach the enemy's ears, but he must have said that he could only guarantee their lives if they moved into an area held by the army in strength.

There was another possibility: in the south was the kingdom of Cogidubnus – could he offer any protection? This is difficult to judge, but at Silchester at least there are substantial defences consisting of two series of earth banks, the inner enclosing $32\frac{1}{2}$ hectares and the enormous outer one of 95 hectares. Both are post-Conquest, since they are aligned to the Roman roads which leave the settlement, almost at the four cardinal points of the compass. Also, pottery of the middle of the first century has been found below the outer bank, and this has suggested that it could well have been constructed at the time of the Revolt.[4] It could further be argued that the large area thus enclosed was necessary for the influx of refugees from London and other settlements in the south-east of the Province.

But the most compelling reason for any flight in this direction would have been Bosham harbour, an alternative escape route across the Channel. Cogidubnus would have given his Roman friends every assistance. Had he joined the rebels, his career would have come to a sudden end, but we know from Tacitus that he lived to a ripe old age and was honoured to its end.[5] Even more significant is the signal honour bestowed on him at some unspecified date, when he was made an imperial legate. It could be argued that this came from his old comrade-in-arms, Vespasian, when he became Emperor, but it could have been earlier if it was for services rendered at this time of crisis. Tacitus must have decided to exclude any reference to this possibility, since it would seem to him irrelevant to destroy the rhythm of his narrative and also, it would have softened the dramatic effect of his description of the London holocaust.

This obvious escape route for the terrified citizens of London also helps to explain why Paullinus could feel little compunction at abandoning the town. In doing so, he had decided, in the crisp words of Tacitus, to save the Province by the sacrifice of a single town. He also deals with this episode with the same economy of words: 'all those left behind were butchered, the British took no prisoners, nor did they consider the money they could get for selling slaves, it was the sword, gibbet, fire and cross' (*caedes, patibula, ignes, cruces*). Dio added details to titillate his readers. Used though we are to horrors and bestialities in our modern world, one still cannot read his words without revulsion. It must, however be appreciated that the Britons were carrying out rites in their sacred groves to fulfil promises solemnly undertaken before the Rebellion started. (The goddess involved was Andrasta, not otherwise known – although there is an Andarta in Gaul – and the word seems to mean 'the unconquerable'.) The women had their breasts cut off and stuffed into their mouths, and long skewers were thrust through their bodies lengthways – a clear sexual allusion. What equally terrifying things they did to the men are not mentioned. Tacitus says, in a very percipient phase, that 'they exacted vengeance in advance' – the effect of the oaths and their fulfilment was to involve everyone in the responsibility for the Revolt. It equally helps to explain the savage vengeance exacted by Paullinus in the name of the Roman god, Mars Ultor, for it was impossible to single out individual culprits, since everyone was compromised.

It must be assumed that Paullinus returned the way he had come, along the main route to the north-west, known much later as Watling Street, Telford's Holyhead Road and, in today's unimaginative signature, the A5. The main body of troops would have been marching their regular twenty miles a day towards the rendezvous selected by the commander. The place would also have been on Watling Street, but at a point which could have been reached without too much difficulty by units stationed in the frontier zone. Here Paullinus would have exercised discretion, since it could have been unwise to risk the concentration of his total command and leave the frontier too bare of troops. His first thought would have been to have with him as many legionaries as possible; he had with him already the full strength of the XIVth and a strong detachment of the XXth, and the only other available legion was IInd *Augusta*. This unit we know now was established at this time in its fortress at Exeter, and an urgent summons was sent for as many cohorts to be despatched as could be spared. The man in command at Exeter was Poenius Postumus, the *praefectus castrorum* or camp prefect. He was third in the command rating, which implies that both the *legatus legionis* and senior tribune were absent and the only place they could reasonably be was with Paullinus, as members of his staff, probably with an odd cohort or two of this legion. Postumus could well have been pinned down in his fortress by the Durotriges, one of the tribes which most probably rose in Rebellion. Whatever the local position may have been, he felt it imprudent to move any of his men as commanded: he may have felt that Paullinus was about to be overwhelmed. In any case it is very unlikely that such a senior officer would have succumbed to fear. The information given by Tacitus at the end of his account, when he was able to add this significant detail, is that Postumus failed to carry out an order and also denied his men glory of the great victory. So he had no alternative but to fall on his sword. One can feel some sympathy for him in his dilemma – to stay in reasonable security, or hack his way 170 miles through hostile country to join the main force which could by then have been annihilated.

The possible sites of the meeting place are Wroxeter, the base of the XIVth, Pennocrucium, where Watling Street joined the road from Chester, or Wall (near Lichfield). Of these, the most likely seems to be the last, since there is a good road from the south along which the IInd *Augusta* was expected to march. There is also supporting archaeological evidence from the site itself which will be considered later. The main body could have reached Wall in five or six days from Anglesey, and probably arrived at the same time as Paullinus riding hard from London.

The Britons would have spent several frenzied days in London, in looting and destruction, apart from their beastly religious rituals. But their thirst for blood had not yet been slaked. When eventually the huge mob began to flow like a great snake along Watling Street, the next objective was a third city, Verulamium, which was just as thoroughly destroyed. This, however, was not occupied by Romans or foreign traders, but by Britons of the Catuvellauni. They suffered because of their strong pro-Roman sentiments, having been rewarded by the status of a *municipium* for their town with a degree of self-government and openings to full citizenship through the magistracy for their leaders. It is likely that some of the tribal notables would have already been given a direct grant of citizenship by Claudius. As we have seen above, the people of the area in all probability were descendants of the Gauls who had migrated in advance of Caesar's conquest of their lands. Although absorbed later by Cunobelinus, they had no affiliations with the Catuvellauni, and would have welcomed the advent of Rome. The rewards they received in consequence only increased the antipathy between them and the older British tribe. But at least the inhabitants of Verulamium would have had time to escape to the north-west and place themselves under army protection. The fact that no skeletal remains have been found is no proof, since bodies would have been collected later and decently buried. Tacitus gives us the figure of 80,000 Roman citizens and allies who fell in the three cities. This seems a gross exaggeration, since in two cases large numbers must have fled, even though the disaster at Camulodunum must have accounted for almost the entire population. It is difficult to believe that the total population of the three places was as much as this figure, and even half might seem excessive.

ROMAN REVENGE

The stories at this point given by Tacitus and Dio vary, the latter historian stating that Paullinus sought to avoid an immediate clash and even became short of food. Had he been able to wait for several weeks, a relief force could have been sent from Gaul or Germany, but it hardly seems feasible that the Britons would have allowed this to happen. Flushed with success, they surely wanted to overwhelm the Roman force by sheer weight of numbers. Paullinus had time only to find the most suitable place to fight a battle on his terms and with his original campaign, so to speak, in reverse. It is possible that he was long distances from his supply bases in Wales, so his men could have been on short rations. His policy would have been to force the Britons to advance as far to the west as possible, to give time for the troops to rest after the forced marches, and to collect reinforcements and supplies. He would not have advanced too far down Watling Street towards the south, but would have kept to the military zone, still expecting to be joined by cohorts of IInd *Augusta.*

The description of the battlefield given by Tacitus is too vague to make identification of the site certain, but there is no reason why we should not accept the factors he lists as a reasonably accurate, probably even an eye-witness, view of the terrain. Paullinus searched for, and chose, the position which gave him the best tactical advantages. It was at the approach to a narrow defile which meant that the Britons were forced to advance into a front of diminishing width: the greater their force, the more packed they would become in their eagerness to reach the Romans. His rear was pro-tected by a wood which prevented any large-scale British infiltration from the rear or outflanking movement. In front was a plain with little or no cover for the Britons: presumably the defile led into this open area, where the main battle would be won. The description suggests a sudden change in the geology from open plain to thick woodland, with a sharp rise in the ground to account for a small valley – though one cannot be sure how much of this would have been due to natural landscape and how much had been changed by clearance and cultivation.

Another factor was the main road along which the Britons would come. Paullinus would have chosen a point somewhere along or very near its line, but it is difficult, as one searches the terrain on the stretch from Wall south-wards, to find a place which closely fits this description by Tacitus. There is, however, a distinct possibility at Mancetter, where a ridge of old hard rock runs in a north-westerly direction, converging on Watling Street near Atherstone. The rise of this steep escarpment of several hundred feet above the flood plain of the River Anker is caused by a fault line, and by the fact that it is composed of quartzite, a rock which has resisted weathering. Unfortunately, it has also attracted quarrymen looking for good-quality stone for roads and ballast. The hillside has been extensively quarried to provide ballast for the railways and top dressing for the streets of the Metropolis in the nineteenth century – which demand has continued to the present day. This activity has changed the shape of the escarpment, but it is still possible to visualise a number of possible defiles which open out to the river plain through which Watling Street runs (Fig. 5). It will never be possible to prove that this was the site of the battle, but, apart from the local topography, there is a military site of this period under Mancetter village, and further discoveries there might perhaps strengthen the case. The evidence, as it stands at present, will be considered below (p. 111).

The essence of the Roman battle plan was the choice of site to give the legionaries the maximum advantage for their close in-fighting tactics. All

F

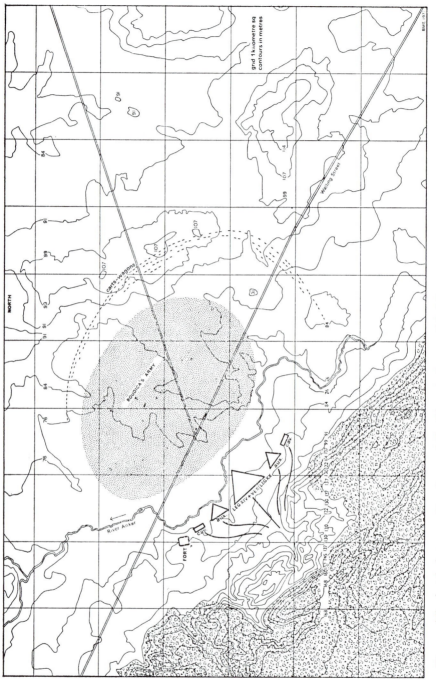

Fig. 5   The battle between Boudica and Paullinus in its possible Mancetter context

that remained was for these tough disciplined soldiers to keep cool and respond quickly and decisively to the commands. While the Romans waited silently in their tight but orderly ranks, the Britons were in a state of wild disorder which their leaders must have found impossible to control. They were a large unruly mob in a state of high exultation, confident of a great victory which would free them from the abominable yoke of oppression and exploitation – so sure of success that they had brought their families by the waggon load to witness the spectacle of Roman slaughter. These vehicles were parked in a great semi-circle round the edge of the battleground, with the women and children sitting on the top for a grandstand view. Dio says that this vaste horde numbered 230,000 which again must be an exaggeration, similar to Tacitus' estimate of British losses at 80,000. If the Roman force consisted of a complete legion, the XIVth and detachments of two others, it could have amounted to between 7,000 and 8,000 legionaries; there also were probably between 4,000 and 5,000 auxiliaries, including the cavalry stationed on the wings. This would make a total of 11,000–13,000 men and the British fighting force could have been as great as 100,000. There was furthermore a large following of women, children and other non-combatants. The odds against the Romans were heavy, but every legionary knew he was worth at least five unarmoured and untrained barbarians.

All the great battle scenes in antiquity had, as we have seen, to be preceded by speeches by the leaders. They were felt by classical writers to be a necessity, since their words were declaimed at public and private gatherings, and a good speech was judged as a piece of rhetoric, for which the educated Roman had a fine ear and judgment. The speech put into the mouth of Boudica, at the outset of the Revolt, by Dio is long and wordy, typical of the exercises invented by teachers and students in the schools of rhetoric in Rome and elsewhere, and totally removed from actuality. Tacitus is very much briefer and to the point, 'The Britons', she declared, 'were used to the leadership of women, but she came before them not as a queen of a distinguished line, but as an ordinary woman, her body cut by the lash avenging the loss of her liberty, and the outrages imposed on her daughters. Roman greed spares neither their bodies, the old or the virgins. The gods were on our side in our quest for vengeance, one legion has already perished, the others are cowering in their forts seeking to escape. They could never face the roar of our thousands, least of all our charge and hand to hand fighting. When the Romans realised their small force and the justice of our cause, they would know it was victory or death', she ended with a strong call. 'This is my resolve, as a woman – follow me or submit to the Roman yoke', at the same time taunting the men to do what she a mere woman was prepared to do. This final plea is packed into seven words by Tacitus with four alliterative Vs for spitting at her warriors – *id mulieri destinatum: viverent viri et servirent.* This is so tight and epigrammatic that most of the translations miss the meaning. But there is a ring of truth in the brisk in-structions issued by Paullinus: 'Ignore the noises and empty threats made by these savages. There are more women than men in their ranks, they have no armour or proper weapons and will break when they feel your steel and sense the courage of men who have beaten them so many times already. What glory lies before you, an elect few who will gather the laurels of a whole army.' This was an exhortation to give his men heart and resolution; then his incisive instructions: 'Keep close order, when you have thrown your javelins, push forward with the bosses of your shields and swords, let the dead pile up, forget all about plunder, win the victory and it's all yours.'

The legionaries stood fast and allowed the Britons to rush about, yelling taunts and hurling missiles to little effect: it must have been unnerving for them to see these still, steel men coldly staring at them with unflinching contempt. With a great blaze of trumpets, the Britons eventually poured into the defile in a solid surging mass. At forty yards the legionaries moved as one and 6,000–7,000 javelins were in the air, quickly followed by a second volley. The first ranks of the Britons fell, as the sharp steel points sank into them; those pressing behind had to climb over them or carry the stricken forward. It was only then that the legionaries flicked their short swords out of their scabbards, and in an easy motion, closed ranks, tucked their heads in and with a great shout charged in wedge formation which drove great clefts into the mass of Britons. Now the Romans had all the advantage. Pushing with their shields, thrusting and twisting their short swords, stamping and trampling over the falling bodies, they heaved and propelled themselves forward. The Britons were so crushed together in this narrow space that they could not use their long swords. As the Romans gained momentum, the sharp wedges drove deeper and deeper into the seething mass of bodies. It was slaughter on a prodigious scale. As soon as the legionaries had broken out of the narrow defile there was room for the cavalry to harry the flanks, and as the Britons broke and ran, to cut them down from behind. But retreat for some was made difficult by the wall of waggons round the plain and the butchery went on, men and women and even the baggage animals.

Tacitus gives us a very brief coherent narrative written for maximum dramatic effect, but he has clearly telescoped the hard hours of gruelling fighting and omitted many significant details. Dio gives Paullinus three speeches of empty rhetoric, but there are indications that some of the words came from the same source used by Tacitus, if not, direct from the *Annals*. But the actual fighting Dio describes as disorganised mêlée, reminiscent of the reliefs on late sarcophagi, with battle scenes packed with writhing limbs and bodies of men and horses. He says that it was only late in the day that the Romans finally gained their victory with many slain or captured alive, while others escaped. The figure given by Tacitus of 80,000 Britons and only 400 Romans slain are hardly credible, unless one halves one and doubles the other at least. Boudica, he says, poisoned herself; but according to Dio, she fell ill and died – maybe another version of the same story.

So Rome won a great victory against heavy numerical odds and *Legio XIV Gemina* covered itself with glory and bore thereafter the honoured title *Martia Victrix*; the XXth too, was present in sufficient strength to be called thereafter *Victrix*, the Victorious. But it was a great shock to the Roman government, for rarely in their annals had there been a rebellion of such magnitude and ferocity. It called into question the policy towards Britain and the need to make a fresh assessment if the Province was to be shaped into the Roman mould. While those responsible for planning and policy-making were pondering over these problems, Paullinus had no such thoughts. Many Roman legionaries had been lost, a whole colony of veterans wiped out and Roman citizens had been massacred and forced to suffer horrific atrocities. The wrath and fury of Rome fell on the Britons, sanctified by the call upon Mars Ultor, the Roman god of vengeance. We are fortunate in having this aftermath recorded by Tacitus (the epitomiser of Dio considered it irrelevant, so it only appears in the *Annals*), since it gives Tacitus an opportunity of accusing Nero of slighting the great hero who had saved Britain for Rome.

THE AFTERMATH

The army was kept in the field (*sub pellibus* i.e. under leather, from which the tents were made), although the winter season was now approaching. Reinforcements were sent from Germany, 2,000 legionaries, eight cohorts of auxiliaries and 1,000 cavalry – 7,000 men in all, which gives some indication of the Roman losses. It has been suggested that the officer in command of this large *vexillatio* was Titus, the elder son of Vespasian and a future emperor, then serving as a senior tribune in Germany.[6] He certainly served in Britain and was well liked, as his biographer records, adding that many statues were erected to him.[7] There seems no other occasion when he could have been in Britain.

Paullinus harried the lands of the tribes which had rebelled or even appeared to be indifferent (*nationum ambiguum*). This created famine conditions. The troops probably seized or destroyed stores and standing crops – though, according to Tacitus, it was the fault of the Britons who had not sown that year but had diverted all their efforts to the Revolt. This seems unlikely for any people so dependent on agriculture, whether they won or lost. There follows a passage made difficult by the loss of some words in the text, but which seems to indicate that the tribes came slowly to a peaceful frame of mind because a quarrel had developed between the Governor and the new Procurator, Julius Classicianus. The latter had advised the Britons to be patient in their sufferings, as the next governor would introduce a new and more pacific policy. At the same time his despatches to Rome begged for the recall of Paullinus, since his unabated passion for revenge was creating so much havoc. As chief financial officer of the Province, Classicianus saw his revenues rapidly draining away.

Nero sent an Imperial freedman, Polyclitus, one of those able Greek Secretaries of State. This gives Tacitus a chance to ride a favourite hobby horse in exposing his contempt for the band of ex-slaves occupying high positions in the government offices under Claudius and Nero. His calculated sneers about the large retinue of Polyclitus which made his progress 'a terror even to our soldiers' and the derision with which he was received by the Britons would have brought rounds of titters in the salons where the *Annals* would be read. Such a passage was also inserted, no doubt, as a welcome relief after the preceding tension and horrors. Tacitus is forced to admit that a reconciliation was effected and both senior officers pacified, but at the first opportunity the Governor was recalled, ostensibly over the loss of a few ships. This may be Tacitus being perverse, since by now his three year term was at an end; in any case, a new policy was needed for Britain. But the historian sees this as the great hero wronged by an effete Emperor, a provincial equestrian and, worst of all, an ex-slave. The new Governor, Petronius Turpilianus, who came to Britain fresh from the consulship in 61, is accused of not asserting himself by further provocation and by giving this spineless inactivity the honourable name of peace – a snide remark most unworthy of the great historian.

The advent of Turpilianus signalled a new attitude towards Britain. Further military action was to cease : no more conquests, no more revenge; reconciliation was to be the order of the day, tact and diplomacy needed to calm the British chiefs and introduce, by more subtle means, the new way of life, a capitalist economy and the concept of urban civilisation. In this new policy, the personality and talents of Cogidubnus were doubtless available to the Governor, nor must the other client ruler be overlooked, for Cartimandua had remained steadfast in her loyalty to Rome throughout the Rebellion. Had she thrown in her lot with Boudica and brought her tribesmen down from the North, Suetonius might not have survived a war on two fronts. But the Queen held back on promises of more wealth and power – or did she perhaps resent the leadership of Britons by another woman? Her fall was yet to come when that bright intellect was clouded by sexual frenzy induced by the youthful Vellocatus, her husband's squire – but that is another story.

6

The Evidence from the Ground

The evidence, which has been accumulating over the last few years, must now be considered and its significance assessed. It would be sensible if this could be arranged in two equal parts, British and Roman, but this cannot be, since very little can be gleaned of the native activities through archaeological means. It is difficult enough to obtain a view of the Iceni and their way of life; the site of the royal palace of Prasutagus is not even known. *The Iron Age Map of Southern Britain*[1] shows the territory of the Iceni as an almost blank area. One is especially struck by the absence of the heavily defended enclosures, such as the hillforts, so prominent elsewhere. The only possibility in the eastern section seemed at one time to be a single ditched enclosure at Tasburgh, near enough to the Roman tribal capital to suggest the royal seat, but recent excavations have produced only Saxon and medieval structures.

This lack of adequate defensive protection has always worried archaeologists, and, in an earlier generation, caused Sir Cyril Fox to argue that the Iceni depended for their safety by restricting access into their territory by means of lengths of dykes, but even these are now considered to be post-Roman in date. The answer must surely be that these fortunate people were not under great threat of invasion or from raiders, except along the Icknield Way on the west side, and here the evidence certainly exists at hillforts like Wandlebury, near Cambridge. Better evidence can be obtained from a study of weapons and wargear of the period, but the problem here is often that of distinguishing between British and Roman where firm dating evidence and associations with identifiable sites are absent.

Celtic and Roman military equipment
A dozen bronzes found at Ringstead, near Snettisham, includes a very fine pair of bridle-bits,[2] and from Westhall (Suffolk) has come a hoard of eight brightly enamelled terret-rings, of the 'crescent' type which is peculiar to eastern Britain,[3] beautifully illustrated in *Archaeologia* at the time of the

discovery.[4] The Westhall hoard was found in a large bronze vessel with other objects, and there is little doubt that it is of the Roman period. The discovery was made in the course of cutting drainage trenches in a field, and there were many signs of occupation and much Romano-British pottery; one cannot, therefore, claim these objects of the pre-Conquest period. The same could be said of another hoard from Saham Toney, between Thetford and Swaffham.[5] This also consists of gaudy examples of enamelled horse gear found at a site which has produced Roman material of the first century; again at Santon, near Brandon, Norfolk, a hoard found as long ago as 1897[6] but has only recently been subject to careful study by Dr Mansel Spratling.[7] Among this interesting assemblage are Roman brooches and fragments of a legionary cuirass (*lorica segmentata*). A stray piece of horse trapping, undoubtedly Roman, said to have been found in the Lakenheath area, is in the Museum at Bury St Edmunds.

These finds raise difficult but fascinating questions about the relationship between the Celtic craftsmen and the Roman conquerors. There are many examples of equipment, especially of horse gear, of undoubted Celtic design and craftsmanship, found on, or near, Roman military sites. When such pieces of metalwork are found in isolation, there is often some doubt as to their origin and a tendency for prehistorians to claim them as Iron Age, while the Romanists may well regard them as having been lost by Roman soldiers. A close study of the decoration, and especially the enamel work, sometimes offers a clue, since Roman taste favoured geometric symmetry, which one rarely sees in Celtic schemes of decoration done for themselves. Thus one of the most famous of all pieces of metalwork, the Battersea shield, in the British Museum, can, because of its almost perfect symmetry, be seen to be made to a Roman order, perhaps as a votive object to be cast as a thanksgiving into the Thames. Another indication is the use of enamel studs in a chequer pattern, a square convention which would have been rejected by the uninhibited flair of a true Celtic craftsman.

An important factor to be remembered is that many of the troops in the Roman army were Celts recruited from the frontier zones, and most of the horsemen came from Spain, Gaul and the Rhineland. These men had no experience of the classical traditions of the Mediterranean and would have delighted in the brightly coloured decorations they could acquire from the British bronzesmiths. It is not surprising to find so much Celtic work in first-century military contexts, made doubtless by the same bronzesmiths who had been providing the British chiefs and their bodyguards with equipment. These workers, like the potters, rapidly adapted themselves to the new market, but their influence was to remain and affect styles in decoration for many years to come.

One fine object which must be considered only to be dismissed as evidence, is the fine decorated cavalry helmet dredged out of the River Wensum at Worthing, some fifteen miles north-west of Norwich.[8] Thought at the time

to have been lost in the round-up of suspects after the battle; it is now recognised as a parade helmet typical of the third century,[9] and must, therefore,
be associated with one of the Saxon Shore Forts.

The military dispositions after the Battle

As the troops poured back into the Midlands from the advanced bases in
the Welsh foothills and mountains, most of the sites they would have
occupied were then old bases, which may in some cases have still been in
military hands, possibly even with a small caretaker garrison. There was no
time at first to build forts. Tacitus tells us specifically that the men were
kept in their campaign bases living in their leather tents. No doubt the old
sweats gave vent to strings of obscenities as they railed against their aristocratic commander in his neglect of the normal rule in all Roman military
operations – that, once the campaign season was over, the troops withdrew
to their winter quarters where they could live in comfort in permanent
barracks. The autumn may not have been especially cold, but it is often
very wet and a tented site can soon become a sea of mud, with water seeping
into the tents. For however carefully drainage channels are cut round them,
until they are all linked up to a system the level steadily will rise and eventually overflow. It may have been, in these miserable conditions, that the
Roman units continued to hunt out fugitives and press on with the destruction of their homes and farmsteads in the name of vengeance. Such savage
action against a defeated enemy soon palls, and for most of the men their
feelings against the Britons would have been quickly satiated. Paullinus did
not do this beastly work himself and could afford to give full play to his
unremitting rage against the rebels, who had had the audacity to challenge
his authority.

It would be satisfying if one could see the archaeological record of such
destruction in East Anglia, but so far none has been found. However, very
little work has been carried out on the native sites and one day perhaps, on
a site which has been protected from the plough and forestation, there
may be the native equivalent of the layer of destruction at the three great
cities. The native buildings would have been entirely of timber, and, without
a bright red layer of burnt daub, the evidence may be difficult or too slight to
offer much hope of interpretation.

The Roman military presence leaves its undoubted mark on the landscape,
and, if Tacitus is correct, one should at least find the campaign bases with
their ditches, enclosures and possibly, under optimum conditions, evidence
of the sites of the tents themselves if the troops found it necessary to dig
drainage ditches, while ovens, latrines and rubbish pits may also be traceable.
Conditions for aerial reconnaissance over East Anglia have not been too
helpful in recent years, since the presence of the large NATO air bases with
their wide approach corridors has severely restricted the private flyer.
Fortunately, the Scole Committee, which organises all the rescue archaeology

for Norfolk, has now a full-time officer for this purpose, and Derek Edwards has been able to add considerably to our knowledge. Even so, Roman military sites are not very common. Two sides and three corners of a 10-hectare marching camp have been recorded at Horstead in the Bure Valley, a few miles north of Norwich (8). Another probable site is at Stuston near Scole just over the border in Suffolk: this is a crop-mark of one positive curved corner and faint indications of another (9). A fort had earlier been postulated in this area based on evidence of some interesting looking ditches, some iron spearheads and an early brooch,[10] but all this is suggestive rather than conclusive. A possible military site was listed by Sir Cyril Fox in his famous survey of the area[11] near Melbourn, nine miles south-west of Cambridge, and an undoubted Roman road known as the Kingsway (p. 175 and map on p. 144). There was visible in the last century a rectangular earth-work of about 200 yards, surrounded by a vallum, with a second vallum towards the east. Although first-century pottery is noted from a nearby cemetery, it seems unlikely that the bank and ditches of a fort of this date would have survived so well.

Apart from Camulodunum, there are, so far, only two sites of permanent forts known in this area. Both have been discovered by aerial reconnaissance, but neither tested with the spade. They had been included as possibilities in 1960, in his study of the archeology of East Anglia, by the late Rainbird Clarke, then Curator of the Norfolk Castle Museum.[12] In 1945, Derrick Riley published a note on a crop-mark of a fort at Ixworth near Pakenham,[13] and further observations by Professor J. K. S. St Joseph made it certain that there is a large fort of seven acres (*c.* 500 ft by 625 ft) on the low-lying meadows south of the village.

Another site which has produced a significant crop-mark is by the Roman settlement of Combretovium (Baylham House) on the road from Camulod-unum, leading due north towards Caistor, the tribal capital of the Iceni. A military identification is indicated by a piece of cavalry equipment which was found when the Roman road was sectioned in 1953–4 by an Ipswich School archaeological society.[14] Pits were found at the edge of the road, containing pottery of the Claudian-Neronian period, and at the bottom of the silt of the roadside ditch came a piece of fretted bronze. This was part of a bronze plate inserted on each side of the saddle cloth to weight it down, and to also provide a decorative feature, especially if it was backed with red leather.

From this area also is thought to have come the remarkable bronze statuette of the Emperor Nero, now in the British Museum, and found in 1795. Twenty-five inches high, it shows the Emperor standing with his left foot resting on what may originally have been a globe, while his right hand is raised to hold a staff or sceptre (5).[15] It is finely made and the cuirass decora-ted with inlaid silver and niello, with large rosettes and sprays of vineleaves. The petals of the rosettes alternate in niello and silver and the eyes of the

Emperor are of the same material, with the eyeball in silver and the pupil niello. The body has been cast in several pieces, the joint between the head and body being visible where the neck meets the cuirass. The arms are also separate, and this explains the absence of his left arm which has dropped or been pulled off. Professor J. M. C. Toynbee has described it as 'suggestive of Nero in the guise of Alexander'.[16] An image of this emperor, who was officially 'damned' after his death, could have been venerated only during his lifetime, and may even have been deliberately broken in AD 68 and discarded, especially if it was one of the official cult images of an army unit stationed here. Such a remarkable object may seem unlikely in a British context. It has been suggested that it was brought into the country after a Grand Tour. Colour was lent to this idea by the fact that it was originally in the possession of the Earl of Ashburnham at Barking Hall, Suffolk. Fortunately, there is a record of the actual discovery in the *Gentleman's Magazine* for 1825,[17] which makes it certain that it came from somewhere near Baylham House, and the mention of a long stone wall near the find spot places it, gives the record some probability.

THE LUNT AT BAGINTON, NEAR COVENTRY

The site, with the strange name meaning 'a wood slope' or 'a high beacon point', stands well above the River Sowe, and looks down towards the thriving city of Coventry, with its enormous car factories mingling uncomfortably with its ancient traditions. During the last war, there were large-scale gravel workings at Baginton which produced enough Roman pottery to indicate the presence of a settlement, some of it dating from the mid-first century. With remarkable prescience, Brian Stanley, a local archaeologist, suggested in 1960 that The Lunt was the site of a Roman fort. Following his hunch, he dug a trench across what turned out actually to be a medieval field boundary, but beneath it he found ditches and a rampart, while in another trench within the defences he located a pit which produced coins and pottery. Thus his postulated Roman fort became a certainty.

It was not, however, until 1966 that further work was possible. By this time the land was owned by the Coventry Corporation, and a long-term policy of excavation and conservation was launched by the City Museum, under the direction of Brian Hobley, the Keeper of Field Archaeology. This enterprise was to develop into a major operation which did not end until 1973, by which date four-and-a-half acres had been stripped and full reports promptly published.[18] The long period of the excavation and the meticulous methods used have given us a most extraordinarily detailed picture of a Roman military establishment which was occupied for only about fifteen years, apart from a late third-century work. This very short span began with the Revolt and ended with the reorganisation of the forces needed for the northern campaigns under Agricola, if not somewhat before. Yet in this

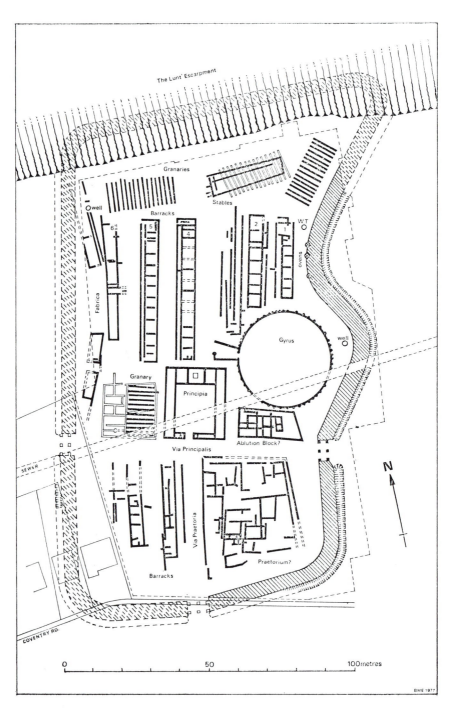

THE LUNT, COVENTRY

period there are at least six phases of rebuilding, three of which were on a drastic scale. This excavation and the careful study of its results has been an object lesson to all those interested in Roman military sites, since it has demonstrated in a highly dramatic form just how complicated these sites are and how misleading could be the results of a few random trenches or the excavation of small areas, which had hitherto been common archeological practice.

Although so much has been done, there are a number of basic questions remaining unanswered. The first period is that of a very large establishment of which the only certain boundary at present is on the north side, where the steep slope precludes any extension in this direction; there is a possibility of the site of the western defences in the undulations of the ground, but excavation has yet to prove this. To the south the pottery found in gravel workings near the church suggests that occupation of this early period could have been extended. So all we have here is the north-west corner of this site with little indication of its extent to the east and south, except that trenches to the east ran into marshy ground, with a thinning out of evidence for buildings, but no sign of any defences. Nor are there any indications of the buildings of this phase or the function of the site. It is not a regular layout and some buildings are at angles to one another. In the historical context it is at this stage that the army was pouring back into central and eastern Britain, to round up the rebels who had fled in large numbers from the battlefield. The central position of The Lunt in relation to the Midland Plain may have been a factor in its choice as a main base fort for the campaign now in full swing to the east and south. It could even have been the Roman campaign headquarters, and main supply base.

The excavator divided the first period into four phases for buildings and rebuilding, and in the last of these there appears a structure unique in Roman military architecture. This has been tentatively christened a *gyrus* (**10**), or training ring for horses, mentioned by the Greek historian Xenophon; there is no known Roman equivalent word. It is a circle of 107.5 ft in diameter, which may have been 120 *pedes Drusiani*, with a wooden wall all the way round, probably standing to a height of eight feet above the ground. The internal surface of the ring had been carefully levelled and covered with sand and gravel. There was a main gated entrance with a funnelled approach, suitable for handling wild or frightened animals. As one would expect, this unique structure has created a great deal of interest and there has been much discussion as to its function. It is generally accepted that it must have been built for animals, and to find an explanation, one must again turn to the historical context.

The Iceni and their allies were now utterly routed, parties of soldiers had searched them out in their homelands, and a terrible vengeance was being carried out under direct orders from the Governor. All portable goods were regarded as spoils of war and, what the soldiers did not take for themselves, were collected and brought into the depots. The bulk of this would have been cattle, grain and other agricultural produce. However, as one of the main sources of wealth of the Iceni was its horses, shown by the fine metalwork from the trappings and harness which have survived, the suggestion is that the Romans found themselves in possession of a large number of these animals – a great windfall for the army, since horses were in constant demand by the mounted units and for traction and as pack animals (although, for the last, mules and donkeys were preferred). The quartermasters had a choice of different breeds for their various functions: for example, the horses used by the crack cavalry regiments (the *alae*) were larger and more powerful than those used by the part-mounted units (*cohortes equitatae*), since the tactics of the latter needed cooperation between horsemen and infantry. If one takes Caesar's descriptions of German cavalry in action as indicating tactics developed by these ethnic units of the Roman *auxilia*, one sees the need for fairly small wiry animals for rapid mounting and dismounting.

All the captured animals would first need to be sorted and graded; any which did not come up to specification or which were unfit, would be rejected and sold into the civil market. The choice horses then had to be subjected to the rigorous training to fit them for their duties in the appropriate type of units. Some animals may have been semi-wild and needed to be broken in before this stage could be reached. On this basic assumption, The Lunt *gyrus* was a corral and arena made necessary by these special circumstances after the suppression of the Revolt. If the site began as the main rearward base for the campaigns against the rebels, it would have been an obvious choice for this task, when units would have been moved forward into the eastern areas to take up their positions in rebel territory. The *gyrus* was built at a late stage in the life of the main base, but already it was in such demand that there was no question of its demolition and rebuilding elsewhere, when it was decided to dismantle the large establishment and concentrate those left behind in a much smaller defended area. Such is the only possible explanation of the extraordinary alignment of the eastern side of the new small enclosure. Instead of taking the normal straight line to form the universal rectangle with its neatly rounded corners, the eastern side has a sinuous course which seemed in the early stages of the excavation to be quite unbelievable, and a great deal of checking and rechecking had to be done before it could be accepted. The subsequent discovery of the *gyrus* made it quite clear that the ditches and rampart had been carefully constructed to accommodate it and so create a bulge in the line.

In short, it presents an anomaly so distressing to the military mind that it may be a pointer to the nature of the new establishment – that it was intended not for a regular unit of the army, but for a group of military horse breakers and trainers. Taking this kind of thinking a stage further, it may not be so surprising that no similar structures have been found inside regular forts, since they most probably belonged only to special kinds of establishments which have yet to be found and studied in areas deep behind the frontier zones. It is interesting that similar lack of military planning is seen in the works depot and compounds at Holt, Denbighshire, the tile works of *Legio* XX and the legionary workshops at Corbridge.

MANCETTER: THE SITE OF THE BATTLE?

The site of the great battle which decided the fate of Roman Britain will never be known for certain, unless some quite remarkable finds are made, such as a mass burial with closely identifiable weapons in association. The ground suggested above, near Atherstone, is the best guess one can make within the limitations of the historical account and the broad strategy of the opposing forces, as we imagine them. This site does at least have the advantage of having a Roman fort in a crucial position at the crossing of the small river Anker. The rising ground and plateau are now occupied by the remnants of a shrunken medieval village, of which all that survives is a fine church and Manor House. William Stukeley saw indications of defences in the eighteenth century, but he did not consider them to be regular enough to be Roman.

In 1955 Adrian Oswald, then Keeper of Archaeology at the Birmingham City Museum, decided to investigate a likely line of ditches behind the Almshouses on the steep slope down to the little river. It is curious that his trench proved, as at The Lunt, that the visible surface feature was a medieval field boundary, but below it he found a ditch containing early Roman pottery.[19] This defensive alignment was explored again in 1968 by Keith Scott and the ditch system was seen to be a rather peculiar one and difficult to interpret.[20] It is not even certain if more than one period is involved: the outer ditch has an almost vertical outer face down to a narrow bottom; above this, on the inner side, is a small notch cut into the clay, probably to take a thorn hedge; while the inner ditch is of a normal type. The position of the ditch system is as near to the river as possible and its pattern seems to indicate the need for a position of great strength – which would have been necessary if this was an anchor point in the battleline extending eastwards to the steep wooded hillside (fig. 5). The Neronian pottery found in the filling of the ditches is of the right period. Another interesting find was made in 1964, when a drain was being laid at the entrance to the Manor House. This was a small hoard of sixteen bronze and copper coins, mainly of the so-called Claudian military imitation issues, and normally associated with the army, as a kind of provisional small change: a soldier buried the contents of his purse and never collected it.

It would be easy to make a romantic story of these discoveries, but the site, like others of this period, is obviously much more complicated than these modest discoveries show. This point has been demonstrated in a dramatic manner. The owner of a house near the Manor decided in 1975 to erect a Victorian lamp-post in his garden, and dug a hole about three feet square. He found no less than three complete *amphorae* laid out on a clay floor. An extension of this small area produced the emplacements where these containers had originally been set upright and a foundation for a timber wall. The owner had by now developed a keen interest in the potentialities of his garden and allowed Keith Scott to open up a large area nearby. A complicated sequence of buildings and pits was found, clearly indicating that the small area was inside a military establishment of three or four main periods. Further work by Keith Scott up to 1991 has been published in summary form.[21]

7

The Trail of Destruction

THE DESTRUCTION OF CAMULODUNUM

Modern Colchester is on the site of the main target for the fury of the rebels, the military colony set up by Ostorius Scapula in AD 48 and the hated citadel of tyranny, the great temple of the deified Claudius. Tacitus mentions other buildings, the senate house (*curia*) which would have been part of the forum and the theatre, and these must have been destroyed. The modern town has been largely rebuilt in the last few years and as large holes were opened up it was possible, in some cases, to observe the deeper Roman layers and structures; more recently, the careful excavation of small areas has been possible. Much, alas, has been lost in the speed of modern commercial development, when time is money and there is little to spare for the past, however interesting it may be to some of us. But we now have a fair amount of evidence of the nature and extent of the savage destruction of 60; when the sites where this has been observed are plotted on a map, an interesting pattern emerges (Fig. 7). The legionary fortress is now known to have occupied the western part of the later *colonia*; when the legionaries left in 48, the defences were levelled down to the top of the timber corduroy in the form of logs laid at right angles and normally laid at the base of the rampart. Some of the military streets were kept in commission, and even buildings seem to have been re-used by the colonists, as at Gloucester.[1] The new *colonia* was planned at its foundation to be larger than the fortress which was about 48 acres, and the extension was towards the east. What is interesting is that the new street plan is at a slightly different angle to that of the military plan. This may have been due to it having to be based on the alignment of the road out of the east gate of the fortress leading to the crossing of the Colne, since there were already buildings erected along it. These included the important religious centre which preceded the temple and this would have determined the angle of the street grid of the eastern part of the *colonia*. Unfortunately, the excavations have not yet revealed the site of the principal buildings of the *colonia*, but it would have been normal practice for the forum to have been built on the site of the legionary

G

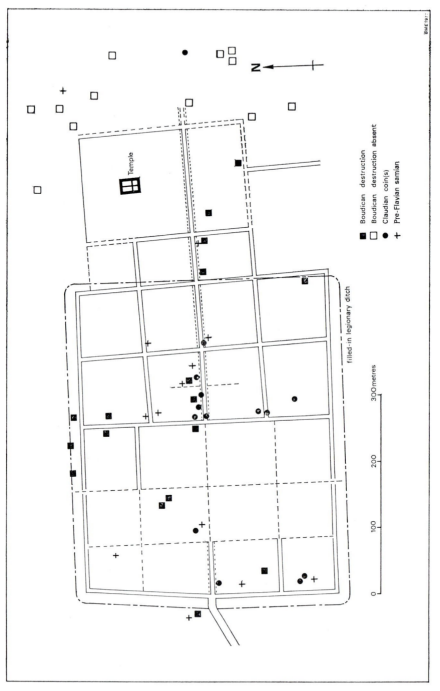

Fig. 7 Roman Colchester: the evidence of the Revolt

headquarters (*principia*). However, it is difficult to postulate this site with the information we have at present about the street plans of both establishments.

The houses of the *colonia* were timber-framed and the spaces between the main verticals filled with wattle and daub, both of which were covered with plaster with painted surfaces. It is possible to study the construction of these buildings in detail, since the wood was partially carbonised in the fire of destruction but even better preserved is the clay infilling which was baked hard. Its fragments bear the clear impressions of the hazel rods of the wattle work. From the Lion Walk excavations came a length of wall large enough to record the decorative lozenge pattern impressed on the clay with a roller stamp to form a key for the wall plaster.

There have been other and more dramatic discoveries. In 1927 a new café was being built on the north side of the High Street and the builders' trenches cut into a great quantity of pottery and glass which poured out of the cutting.[2] A further excavation two years later produced more; when studied, the collection was found to include fragments of several hundred samian vessels, many of the factory of Primus, colour-coated bowls and jars imported from Central Gaul, lamps and masses of fine thin but colourless glass. The most extraordinary vessel is a very rare type of drinking cup known as a rhyton, in the form of a grotesque head with a large mouth from which one drank. There was evidently a pottery and glass shop along the main street of the *colonia*. Another pottery shop was found in 1927 on the other side of the street on a site adjacent to the Red Lion; large pieces of about seventy decorated bowls were recovered and it is evident that only a small number of potters is represented. This means that, as with the shops at the Cups Hotel, the pottery was stored in crates received directly from the factories of Felix, Aquitanus, Licinus and Mommo.

When the Cups Hotel was rebuilt in 1974, it gave an opportunity of examining an adjacent site where the lower courses of a wall were still found standing; it consisted of timber framing with brick infilling and the intensive heat had reduced the upright timbers to carbon. Inside the building deposits of burnt seeds were found and studied by Peter Murphy at the Department of Archaeology, University of Southampton. They turned out to be mainly of *emmer*, a species of wheat, but of poor quality. Seeds of bread wheat were also present, together with a few weeds, vetch, corn cockle and brome grass. Another sample was almost entirely seeds of flax and gold of pleasure, a weed usually found with it. The small size of the flax seeds suggests that the plant was cultivated for its fibres rather than its oil. The Lion Walk excavation in 1973 produced burnt fruits including dates (**14**) which were probably imported in *amphorae*, and there was also a plum. Further excavations on the site of the pottery shop by the Red Lion produced some burnt olives. On the same site, Philip Crummy found the remains of a charred bed with pieces of wood, cloth with a diamond twill and other weaves, and a mass of stuffing – all of which, it was thought, constituted two thin mattresses covered with cloth.[3]

Curiously enough, few human remains have been found of the unfortunate people who perished in the holocaust. A skeleton in the destruction deposit on the site of the Telephone Exchange appeared to have been hacked about, but it can be presumed that most of the bodies would have been recovered and decently cremated as an act of piety. In the adjacent *insula* (No. 10) the fire had actually scorched the surface of the Roman street and burnt out a timber-lined gully.[4] The debris from the area also produced fragments of lamp moulds, indicating that they were being manufactured in Camulodunum at this time. During the building of the original Telephone Exchange in 1926–7, it was not possible to arrange for archaeological observation, but casual finds were brought into the Museum and these included a hoard of twenty-seven coins which had been burnt and had been in a small vessel. There are bronze issues of Claudius and represent a cache of small change of one of the colonists.[5]

THE TEMPLE OF CLAUDIUS

The great temple itself has produced very little evidence of the destruction, mainly since no large-scale excavations have been undertaken and the temple itself was totally encapsulated in the Norman Castle traditionally believed to have been built by Eudo in 1076, when it was thought to be the palace of King Coel. It was not until 1920 that the Roman structures were studied and identified by Wheeler and Laver.[6] It is tragic that a monument of such outstanding importance to the Province of Roman Britain has been encroached upon by development in recent years and only the most hurried and scanty investigations permitted. This has especially applied to the ornamental south *temenos* or boundary wall and the massive entrance to the sacred precinct. Two hurried investigations, one by M. R. Hull in 1953[7] and the other by Max Hebditch in 1964,[8] are tantalising in revealing how much was there to be opened up and studied. The whole of this area up to the edge of the Castle ditch should have been acquired and added to the Castle Park for the better public appreciation of this centre of the Imperial cult in Britain – but, as usual, commercial profit took precedence over the public good. The original scheme for the boundary of the sacred precinct was an open arcade, but it is not yet certain from the excavations whether this was built before or after 60. M. R. Hull reported that the road side drain in front of the arcade was built of tiles but included blocks of alabaster and Purbeck marble which had been subject to the intense heat. Max Hebditch found that Purbeck marble had also been used, but he regards this drain as much later and associated with another fire at the end of the second century, replacing the earlier sequences of timber-lined drains. So what exactly had been completed and was standing in 60 is still open to question.

In the more recent work, fine moulded white plaster was found below the earliest street, and elsewhere similar fragments have been clearly connected with the burnt-clay blocks of the destruction.[9] So it seems possible that in 60 work was still in progress in the temple itself and that the building of the precinct and its surrounds was yet to start.

During the years 1930–5, one of Britain's earliest rescue digs was organised at Colchester in advance of the ring road which passed over the Sheepen area, which lies to the west of the *colonia*, on the ground which slopes gently down to the River Colne. The site proved to be very rich in finds belonging to an industrial area contemporary with the fortress and early *colonia*. At that time, it was mistakenly thought to be the centre of the British capital, which now seems more likely to be situated in the Gosbecks area. Whatever was standing here in 60 was destroyed and the debris resulting from this was rich in fragments of metal working, such as ironwork and bronze clippings. The excavators concluded there had been an intensive effort at the last moment to equip the aged colonists with battle gear by hastily repairing weapons and armour, by now rusty with disuse. There were many pieces of helmets, shields and buckles, and iron fragments from legionary body armour (*lorica segmentata*). One particular pit (A.21) was 'a small hollow filled with ash and charcoal, which spread for some distance round it [in which] were a mass of iron helmets and fragments, together with bronze fittings, apparently dumped there in a sack'. It is interesting to note that these helmets all conform to the same Imperial-Gallic type like those found at Mainz, which were coming into service about the time of the invasion of Britain, and by 60 had become well established.

The most spectacular of all the evidence of the fury of the rebels is in the form of two tombstones of serving soldiers. They belong to an early military cemetery about half a mile along the road which left the west gate of the fortress in a south-westerly direction. The standing tombstones were smashed down and two of them were found lying face down where they had fallen. One, discovered in 1868, is a stone commemorating a centurion, Marcus Favonius Facilis, of the *Legio* XX. It had been broken into two pieces and must have fallen near its original position, since only three feet away was found a lead cylinder containing the burnt bones (presumably) of Facilis, a small phial (doubtless for a perfume to be poured into the grave), and a small thin walled cup with a green lead glaze[11] from a factory in the Allier Valley of Central Gaul. The stone had been set up by two men, Verecundus and Novicius who, as *liberti*, had probably been slaves freed under the terms of their master's will. On the upper half of the Bath stone is a finely executed relief showing the rather grim-faced centurion, his left hand on the pommel of his sword swinging elegantly at his left side, whilst in his right hand is the vine stick (*vituus*), the symbol of his office, like the modern officer's swagger cane. The relief gives us splendid details of his equipment: the broad belt with its highly decorated panels, his cuirass probably of fine mail with extra protection at the shoulders from a pair of plates, his skirt with two rows of pleats probably made of hardened leather strips (since no metal plates of this design have ever been found) and his cloak is draped over his left shoulder and arm. He wears greaves to protect his knees and shins, this being made necessary since he rides a horse on the march. He affects a hair style of the period similar to that on the bronze head of Claudius and his ears project also in the fashion of the date. It is a remarkable monument, one of only a few we can match with the large collection from the Rhineland. Above all it gives us the only piece of evidence which positively identifies the legion stationed here in the early days of the Conquest.

Another stone from the same cemetery was not discovered until 1928, during some building work a little to the west of the findspot of Facilis, but in the same alignment and just south of the Roman road. This monument commemorates an auxiliary officer with the rank of a *duplicarius*, i.e. he had double pay and belonged to the First *Ala* of Thracians, a crack cavalry regiment which came to Britain with the invasion army. It had been raised in Thrace prior to this, so it is not surprising to find that, although his name is the fairly common Roman one of Longinus, his father's name is purely native and Slav-like, Sdapezematygus. He came from the district (*pagus*) of Sardica, which is the modern city Sofia or Sofiya, the capital of Bulgaria. He was forty years old when he died and had served for fifteen years – an older recruit than was usual, but this must have been due to the way in which the unit was first created. The top of the stone has a pair of lions, holding snakes in their paws and flanking a sphinx, which would normally have had the hindquarters and legs of a bird, but here is given human-like knees. All these are typical classical symbols of death, the sphinx and the lion as devourers, and the snake of life after death. The officer himself rides proudly on his horse, much larger than those used by the part-mounted units (*cohortes equitatae*). It could have been fourteen hands, but on the stone the length of the animal has been compressed to fit the space; one can, however, get an idea of its size by comparing its head and neck with the rider.

This stone is unusual in showing the horse in a static position instead of galloping over the fallen foe. The Britons might have been enraged at this portrayal of an enemy of Rome and this could well account for the smashing of the face of Longinus and the blow on the horse's nose before the stone was tipped over. The strange cowering figure with the round shield is more like an animal than a human being, and is reminiscent of a popular image in this country of the Japanese during the last war. It is not, however, intended to show the Roman soldier supreme over the conquered foe, but is another symbol of death and the ultimate victory. Longinus himself is worthy of study. He sits with such confidence on his saddle-cloth, but, of course, without the stirrups which were much later to revolutionise cavalry. He wears a cuirass of large scales (*lorica squamata*) over his tight-fitting leather breeches and raises aloft his oval shield in the left hand. His right originally carried a lance or javelin which was made of bronze and fastened into a hole in his hand, as on Trajan's Column; but this would have been wrenched out and cast away when the rebels wrecked the stone. The horse is beautifully groomed and its trappings decorated with large circular ornaments from which cloth or leather streamers flutter, matching doubtless the fringes on the saddle-cloth. The carving is very crisp and unweathered, but no traces of the gesso surface over the rough stone surfaces of the background have been noted.

There would have been other burials and their monuments in this small cemetery which would have suffered the desecration. There has, however, never been a large-scale excavation of this interesting area, although boys of the Grammar School, under the direction of A. F. Hall, did some trial holes in 1934 and 1940, mainly to trace the road. They also investigated a small walled cemetery at a later date.[12] This plainly indicates that the area continued in this use, although the Grammar School lies to the west of the early military cemetery. The broken condition of the wrecked stones may account for the fact that no attempt was made to reinstate them. This particular spot appears to have been under military care, since there is the stone of another legionary whose name is missing. The fragment gives part of his career[13] which includes service with **XX** *Valeria Victrix* which places its date after 60 when this legion received the title. The stone is of Purbeck marble which ceased to be used for outdoor use by the end of the first century, since it weathers so badly.

This applies equally to another monument to an auxiliary of the same material (*RIB*, 205). This is a tantalising fragment of the left-hand edge only, but there is just enough to suggest very strongly that he belonged to the *Coh I Vangionum*[14] which was a *cohors equitata*, i.e. part-mounted, but there is nothing to indicate whether he was a serving soldier or not. It was found in Balkerne Lane in 1889, just outside the fortress, but could, of course, have been moved from its original position for use as building material. The possibility of auxiliaries being present here in the early years need cause no surprise since, in this period of Claudius and Nero, it is common to find forces of mixed units in forts, Hod Hill being a good example; the practice of having single units in forts appears in Britain to begin with the Flavian dynasty. It would also have been surprising if Ostorius Scapula had taken away a legion and left no troops at all at Camulodunum. There could have been an auxiliary fort on a site yet to be found to protect the first colonists, and its troops transferred to the frontier zone perhaps under Veranius in his big push into Wales in 56. But this must remain speculative.

Apart from the stones, there have been many finds from graves and the collection in the Museum which is most relevant is that made by George Joslin, from about 1870 to 1890, when he owned the land in the area of the military cemetery, and carried out excavations of his own. There are six grave groups which predate 60 : the most fascinating is No. 3, thought to be of a child. It contained thirteen vessels, thirty-six coins (eleven of Agrippa and twenty-five of Claudius), two glass bottles and a number of small phials, a bronze skillet, and objects of bone, damaged in the cremation but recognisable as combs, cups and caskets. The weirdest is a collection of twenty-one pipe-clay figurines. Four are elderly, three men and one woman, reclining as if round a feast, while another four are reading from scrolls, and a figure, presumably a slave, is waiting on them.[15] It looks like an absurd caricature of a group of old colonists dining, but are they really children's toys? The wealth of the grave goods makes it more plausible that they belong to a colonist whose old comrades in arms wish to immortalise the happy hours they had passed together eating, drinking and listening to interminable stories of past campaigns. The date of the pottery in the grave puts it before 60, so it might be post-military, in which case the colonists had taken over the cemetery, naturally regarding themselves as still part of the army.

THE DESTRUCTION OF LONDON

Digging in London has always been more difficult than any other British city because there has been a greater intensity of occupation and rebuilding. Whereas one normally reaches Roman levels eight to ten feet below present ground level, in London one has usually to go down to twenty feet. One hopefully excavates in this city at great cost to this depth, only to find, almost invariably, that a very small fraction of the area has any surviving Roman levels. They often stand up like oddly shaped monoliths between vast medieval rubbish pits and more recent cess-pits and wells. It is a wonder that anything can be gained at all, and one has great sympathy with the archaeologists trying to make much out of so little; but there is always the hope of finding an area like that of the temple of Mithras, which escaped the worst of the interference. There has been a tendency to attribute any signs of destruction and human remains to Boudica – as, for example, the large number of detached skulls found in various places in the bed of the Walbrook.[16] But only careful examination to determine if the head has actually been severed from the body, and Carbon 14 determinations, will help to place these grisly remains in a historical context.

Fortunately, firmer evidence can be gleaned by other means, as was discovered by Gerald Dunning while he was the Investigator of Building Excavations in London. He examined the Roman pottery in the Guildhall Museum, London, and noticed that some kinds of pottery, in particular the samian table wares imported from Gaul, had turned black when subjected to considerable heat. This could occur when sherds came in contact with hearths or furnaces, but he observed that there were large pieces of bowls and other vessels which were unlikely to have been broken and discarded as rubbish, but had been burnt as whole pots in a fire which consumed the buildings in which they were kept. These vessels fall into well defined chronological groups and Gerald Dunning realised that he was looking at collections of Roman pottery from large-scale fires which had swept across much of the City. One of these, the earliest, is obviously that caused by the destruction of Londinium by the Britons when they swept down on the unprotected community.

He then plotted the findspots of the burnt samian and also collected all the evidence of extensive burning he could find in old reports.[17] In 1930, for example, a layer of clay, turned bright red in the heat, was noticed in George Yard, Lombard Street; from it came the unusual samian form 11, a crater derived from an earlier Arretine shape and of Claudian-Neronian date. At Lloyds Bank a little hoard of seventeen fire-damaged coins of Claudius had been found. In all he records thirteen examples, three of them with burning *in situ*, and the rest in the form of burnt samian with a secure provenance. There are indications too of an east-west road of this early period, more or less under Lombard Street itself. Since then the number of these findspots has increased as the map shows (Fig. 8). In 1950, a burnt layer was observed at St Swithin's House to the west of the Walbrook with a pit into which the burnt material had sagged and a complete *amphora* was recovered.[18] Faint indications of early timber buildings have been noticed below the great Governor's Palace,[19] which must have dominated the view of the City from the river in later times; and excavations in 1972 by Hugh Chapman at Aldgate[20] produced a destruction layer with burnt buildings and Neronian pottery, proving a roadside development on the route to Camulodunum.

Gerald Dunning's original conclusions still hold good. The nucleus of the earliest Roman settlement was a bridgehead at the crossing of the Thames at London Bridge and on the hill slope east of the Walbrook. The spread of finds beyond this seems to have been along the two main roads – that to the north-east towards Camulodunum, passing by what later became Aldgate, and that to the north-west towards the Newgate and Ludgate of medieval times, thence to Verulamium and Silchester and beyond. It is a small area, perhaps only a third of that encircled with defences at the end of the second century, and, as one might expect, concentrated on the bridge and river with its wharfs and warehouses.

VERULAMIUM

As the mass of Britons straggled along Watling Street, sated with their destruction and blood-letting, they passed through the city of Verulamium. Unlike the other two centres, Camulodunum and Londinium, this was entirely a British settlement in the territory of the Catuvellauni. Yet it was

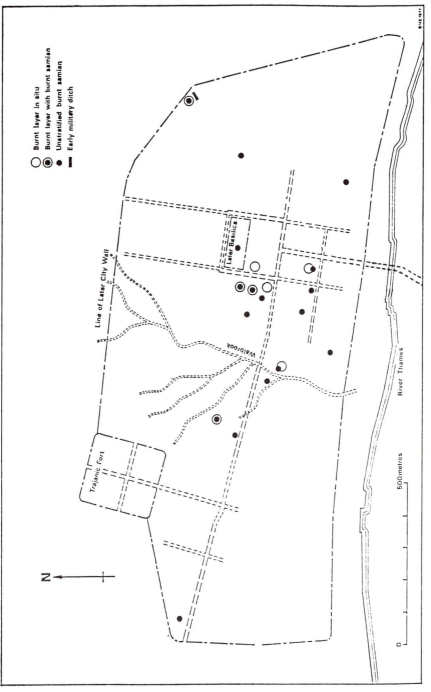

Legend:
- ◯ Burnt layer in situ
- ◉ Burnt layer with burnt samian
- ● Unstratified burnt samian
- ▌ Early military ditch

Trajanic Fort

Line of Later City Wall

Later Basilica

Walbrook

River Thames

N

0   500metres

Fig. 8 Roman London: the evidence of the Revolt

as thoroughly and savagely destroyed as the other two. Why was so much hatred and vengeance poured out against these particular Britons?

As we have seen, the deep division between these groups of Britons of the south-east stems from their origins. The people of the Verulamium–Welwyn–Braughing area had fled from Caesar's advance in Gaul, had settled and became one of the richest communities in Britain. They were eventually absorbed into the territory of their old enemies, the Catuvellauni, whose original centre was probably somewhere in West Essex. They probably resented this through several generations and welcomed the Romans in AD 43, giving them considerable help. In return for this Claudius raised the status of their town to that of a *municipium*. The only direct evidence for this comes from Tacitus, and there are scholars who have considered that he was using the term loosely, so that it cannot be certain that the city was given a charter by Claudius or Vespasian (assuming in the case of the latter Emperor, that Tacitus was wrong in stating that it was a *municipium* by 60). However, the extensive excavations, first by Sir Mortimer Wheeler,[21] and later by Professor Frere, have shown that Verulamium is unusual among the towns of Roman Britain, in having a foundation as early as *c*. 50, with a degree of sophisticated planning and construction work which suggests direct military aid. The Forum, too, is not only larger but quite different in plan from those in Britain and more akin to the Gallic types. But only part of the plan is known to us, since the centre is covered by St Michael's church and vicarage.

In 1955, three fragments of a large inscription on Purbeck marble were found when a bulldozer was levelling an area for the playground of a school.[22] It tells us that the Forum was completed late in AD 79 during the governorship of Agricola, so it must have been started at least five years earlier, depending on the speed of construction. This building could have been a total replacement of an earlier Claudian structure. The inscription, although very fragmentary, can be almost completely restored, since the first four lines consist of Imperial names and titles which were restricted to known formulae, and when set out is seen to have been at least 13ft wide. It is in the bottom two lines where serious difficulties in interpretation arise, since they give information about the particular building and circumstances of the dedication. The upper of the two lines contains the name of the Governor and although there are only four letters . . .]GRIC[. . . there is no possible doubt that they are part of the name of the most famous of all the governors of Britain, Gnaeus Iulius Agricola. The last line is the most infuriating, since there are two letters, VE, followed by an upright on the very edge of the fragment which could equally well be an L or an R. This presents two possible alternatives, either CATV]VEL[LAVNORVM or VER[VLAMIO. The former would have referred to the name of the *civitas* and the latter to the name of the city as a *municipium*. Another quarter of an inch would have given us the exact status of the town and resolved all the arguments. The line ends with the letters . . .]NATA which also presents a problem, but of lesser significance; they could be expanded as either DO]NATA or OR]NATA; one will just have to wait until more fragments of this crucial inscription are found.

The excavations, which started in 1955 under the direction of Professor Sheppard Frere, were made necessary by the construction of a new road across the Roman City. It runs between the Forum and the temple, with its associated theatre, and involved extensive excavations of three *insulae* XIV, XXVII and XXVIII. The first report of this was published by the Society of Antiquaries of London in 1972.[23] Over the whole of this area a layer of destruction was found at least a foot thick, consisting of burnt daub and ash. It was even possible to suggest that the wind blowing at the time of the destruction came from the south-west, sweeping the flames along the main street in front of the Forum. The timber buildings fronting the street are identified as shops linked together at the front by a colonnade – an interesting example of a piece of civic planning one might expect from the municipal status of the City. There are no striking discoveries like those at Camulodunum, but it was possible to study interesting minor details, such as the plank flooring of some of the rooms, and there were several pits sunk into the floors which may have been for storage. The pieces of coke-like organic material which had melted were difficult to identify, but it was thought they could have been wool or hair of garments. One room had been a bronze-smith's workshop, and there appeared to be a series of shallow trays for catching the waste from lathes washed down by water drips. There were no portable valuables or traces of human remains, so it can be concluded that the inhabitants had time to remove themselves and their portable wealth to places of safety before the rebels appeared, and it is also clear that the citizens had expected such treatment.

Some of the wealthy citizens, who were also landowners, had by 60 started to develop their estates near the City, and build country houses on the classical model. Fragments of such a building have been found below the later villa at Gorhambury, during rescue excavations carried out by David Neal.[24] This villa is virtually on the outskirts of Verulamium and the fragments of timber buildings destroyed by fire at this date seem to be part of two courtyards with rooms round them over a strip at least 35 yards long. Although these discoveries cover a small area, there is enough to give a glimpse of classical planning. It is unusual to find villas constructed at this early date in Britain, and it must reflect the new status of Verulamium. There may have been a desire on the part of some of the Britons, who could have received grants of citizenship, to demonstrate their affiliation to Rome, by adopting wholeheartedly the new mode of living now open to them, and indeed expected of them by their Roman masters. Nothing could have more roused the fury of the rebels than this ostentatious display of philo-Roman sentiment.

THE BRONZE HEAD OF CLAUDIUS

In the spring of 1907, a youth mudlarking in the bed of the River Alde at Rendham, near Saxmundham in Suffolk, found a full size bronze head of the Emperor Claudius (6). It was exhibited at the Society of Antiquaries of London on 3 December 1908,[25] by the Victorian Royal Academician, Sir Lawrence Alma Tadema, famous for his enormous canvasses of classical scenes with their inevitable, partially draped females. His great interest in the classical world is apparent from his meticulous attention to detail in all his paintings, and from his large collection of photographs of classical sculptures and monuments now in the Birmingham University Library. The head passed into the hands of the landowner, and only quite recently was it acquired by the British Museum. There now seems little doubt about its identification as that of Claudius, although the workmanship is provincial. The most significant points about the bronze is that it had received a severe blow at the back and that the jagged edges at the neck clearly establish that it was violently hacked from the body. So, it was not just a bust, but a full-size statue which had suffered this damage. His eyes, now open holes, but originally filled with life-like enamel or glass, seem to be looking into the far distance and this has led to the suggestion that it was part of an equestrian statue.[26] Others have held it to have been the cult statue itself from the Temple of Camulodunum, but this surely would have been larger and the workmanship of finer quality. It was no less a scholar than Haverfield who first stated that it was probably loot from the sacking of the *colonia*.[27] Such a statue could well have graced a public building or open space, and what a splendid trophy the head would have made – carried on a pole to have mud and rubbish thrown at it by the triumphant jeering mob. Later, when the rebels were on the run, it would have been a hot piece to have in one's possession, so was thrown into the river, or was it a votive deposit? – to be fished out 1,847 years later by an astonished young man.

THE HOCKWOLD TREASURE

What could also be considered as loot from the sack of Camulodunum is a hoard of silver found at Hockwold-cum-Wilton in Norfolk, on the edge of the Fens. It consists of five double-handled wine cups and two bowls, but the handles and bases have been broken off and one of the bowls crushed into a flat mass of metal[28] (18, 19). Some of the vessels had beautifully incised decorations of ivy leaves and musical instruments; one of the cups, which has been badly flattened, is decorated with relief *repoussé* work and with vine and olive sprays bound together; the workmanship is very fine and somewhat unusual. The cache is obviously loot and, although it cannot be precisely dated, falls into the early post-Conquest period. These fine wine cups and bowls might well have graced the table of a wealthy colonist. It would be difficult to place them in an earlier historical context, unless they were from the royal Icenian household, hastily buried when the Roman soldiers treated Boudica and her daughters with such indignity and contempt. But it is too small a cache for this, and is more likely to have been the result of theft or loot.

THE HAWKEDON HELMET

An object which can be associated with the Revolt with some confidence is a very heavy bronze helmet (24), ploughed up in 1965 at Hawkedon, Suffolk, some ten miles north of Lavenham.[29] Now in the British Museum, it is of thick bronze with traces of tinning on the surface and weighs over five and a half pounds. Its weight and appearance identify it as a helmet used by gladiators, but, as Kenneth Painter has suggested, not for fighting in the arena, but for practice. A maker's mark reads OS with the S reversed in the Etruscan manner, which may indicate a Campanian origin and date to the first century. The helmet has received severe damage on the right-hand side, as if from a heavy blow. Evidence of gladiators in Britain is not very strong, but their portrayal on glass, pottery and mosaics shows that they must have been popular, although of course their use in Britain may have been limited. The most likely time and place to have found them is in the middle of the first century, at the veteran settlement at Colchester, where games and shows must have been regular events, associated with the ritual of the Imperial cult centred in the great temple dedicated to the deified Claudius. The emperors jealously guarded the right to hold the largest and most magnificent shows in Rome, and keep an eye on those in the provinces to make sure there was no danger of competition. For they were worried in case a wealthy official or citizen began courting popularity by being overlavish with spectacles of this kind. To counter this, Claudius transferred the authority of holding shows from the provincial governors to more junior officers of the status of *quaestors*. At Camulodunum, apart from the needs of the Imperial cult administered by the *severi augustales*, a group of the most important citizens of the Province, the *colonia* itself would have had special religious ceremonies every five years from the foundation. This would have been the responsibility of the magistrates elected for these occasions, known as the *quinquennales*.[30]

Like the head of Claudius, the helmet was probably looted from the *colonia* stores and could even have been used in battle by one of the Britons. There are examples of the actual use of gladiators in warfare, as in the Gallic revolt of Sacovir in AD 21,[31] apart from the famous slaves' revolt of Spartacus. Heavy and cumbersome as it was, it offered splendid protection for anyone strong enough to wear it for any length of time; in this case it must have been a rebel who survived the main battle, and fled homewards, to be hunted down in the savage reprisals which followed.

THE TOMBSTONE OF CLASSICIANUS

Perhaps the most striking and evocative of all the surviving traces of the great Revolt is the spectacular sepulchral monument of the Procurator, Gaius Julius Alpinus Classicianus (**23**). It is rarely possible to make such a direct equation between the historical account and the archaeological evidence. To Tacitus, he was an equestrian who interfered with the course of justice and denigrated his great hero, Suetonius, but this, as we have seen above, was a very narrow partisan view. Classicianus died in Britain probably while still in office, and this fine monument was put up by his wife in one of the cemeteries on the east side of Londinium, probably in the area of the Minories and Goodman Fields. Late in the fourth century, like many other large monuments, it was dismantled and the great blocks of limestone used for the building of the projecting bastions on to the city wall.

In excavations for cellars of a house in Trinity Place in 1852, on a plot of land which backed on to the face of the Roman wall, the south face of a projecting bastion was uncovered and demolished; about forty cart-loads of stone were taken away, consisting of large blocks, broken cornice mouldings and column drums (**22**). Among them was a first-century tombstone of Aulus Alfidius Olussa, an Athenian, who died at the age of 70[32] and a slab over five feet long and two-and-a-half feet high, bearing three lines of an inscription, the first two being DIS MANIBVS (to the Shades of the Underworld) and the third giving the name of Classicianus. Another fragment was a piece of a bolster, one of a pair normally found supporting the 'focus', or the dish found on the top of an altar into which libations was poured. From this it is apparent that the Procurator's monument was in the shape of a large altar, a form popular in the Rhineland. Much of this fine stretch of Roman wall, so acutely observed by Roach Smith,[33] was destroyed in 1882 for the building of the Inner Circle Railway, but no more stones of the monument were found at this time. In 1935, the new station of Mark Lane was built, later to be named Tower Hill. The excavations uncovered the north face of the bastion, the other side of which was seen by Roach Smith in 1852. This time the surviving three courses of the structure were carefully cleaned by Frank Cottrill, who at that time was Investigator of Excavations in London employed by the Society of Antiquaries.[34] Another part of the inscription was seen lying upside down, as part of the bottom course (**20**). It included three lines of letters from the base of the inscription and put beyond doubt the argument that the monument was that of the Procurator associated with the Revolt. This still leaves at least two lines in the middle of the inscription which would have included his career, but the stones on which these would have been cut now seem unlikely ever to be found. The full inscription now recovered reads:

DIS
M]ANIBVS
C.IVL.C.F.FAB.ALPINI.CLASSICIANI
....
....
PROC.PROVINC.BRITA[NNIAE
IVLIA.INDI.FILIA. PACATA. I[NDIANA
VXOR [F

When grants of citizenship were made in the early Empire, it was the practice to assume the voting tribe of the patron who made the grant. The Fabian tribe was that of Julius Caesar and Augustus, so it is reasonable to infer that the family became citizens at this date, and Classicianus could have been the grandson of the first in the line. His name indicates a Rhineland origin, probably Trier. The family became sufficiently wealthy to join the equestrian class, which supplied the candidates for high positions in the government service, such as provincial procurators and regimental commanders in the *auxilia*.

His wife, Iulia Pacata Indiana, was the daughter of Iulius Indus, who helped the Romans in the revolt of Florus in AD 21 against injustice and heavy taxation. Tacitus records (*Annals*, III, 42) his successful intervention at the head of a local militia which, possibly as a reward, became a regular auxilia cavalry regiment, named after Indus. This unit the *Ala Indiana Gallorum* served in Britain at the time of the Conquest and the tombstone of one of the troopers, Dannicus,[35] has been found at Cirencester. Iulia Pacata survived her husband and her name appears on a fragmentary inscription found near Trier in, or before, the seventeenth century, but since lost, which could have been from her own tombstone or from that of a member of her family.[36] The monument to Classicianus has been restored and is now in the British Museum (23), although, from the size of the lettering, it is probable that it was much larger and even more imposing. Nevertheless, it remains the most important surviving memorial to the great Revolt.

Epilogue

This dramatic but intensely tragic revolt had a profound effect both on the Britons and on Roman Imperial policy towards their new province.

For many of the Britons it was the end of the road, for, with the destruction of the Druidic centre on Anglesey, the strong anti-Roman faction with its links with all the tribes was shattered and was never able to re-group. With this all hopes vanished of a Roman defeat and withdrawal. Those survivors who possessed strong convictions doubtless lived out their remaining years as sullen, embittered individuals, but the new generations grew up with quite different ideas: the acceptance of the Roman presence, and with it, the beginnings of the appreciation that the Romans were part of a vast community with trading links stretching to the very limits of the known world. The year AD 60 was a watershed for many Britons, since up to this moment there was a real possibility that somehow the Roman Government might be persuaded to give up its conquest. The number of people who held on to this hope may have been few, but they were the tribal leaders, and thus the most influential. Their active participation in the Revolt led to their deaths, either on the battlefield or in the subsequent relentless pursuit. The Revolt had brought all the native hostility to the surface, and few of its leaders are likely to have survived. For the great mass of peasants, it was probably never more than an exchange of one set of masters for another. Thus, after two or more generations, it is hardly likely that there would have been any Britons living in the Province prepared to question Roman authority, although there may have been many causes for grievance inherent in the system.

The Roman Government was no stranger to serious native revolts. Having conquered Gaul with such oustanding speed and brilliance, Caesar almost lost it in the great rising under Vercingetorix, and a lesser man would have failed. The Thracians rose in 11 BC, and it took three years of tough fighting before Calpurnius Piso crushed the tribes. Much worse than these was the great rebellion of AD 6 when Dalmatia and Pannonia both rose at the same time but, fortunately for Rome, not in a combined operation; and even the

H

great military experience of Tiberius and five legions was inadequate to deal with them. Eventually, more troops were summoned from the East and with an army of 100,000 he was able to restore Pannonia to order in AD 7–8, after which he turned on the Dalmatians.

The experience in Britain was different and more traumatic, since it involved the total destruction of three cities, including a veteran settlement, and this struck at the very core of the deeply held concept of Rome's destiny in spreading her greatness and urban civilisation into a barbarian world. Losses of men in battle and even whole settlements of traders was a common and acceptable occurrence, but the holocaust in Britain went well beyond this and must have sent a shock wave of horror and outrage through the governing circles in Rome. Questions were raised about the civilising policy towards the new province: why, they would have asked, after almost twenty years of occupation have the Britons suddenly and so viciously turned against us?

It was a time for reassessment. An enquiry was needed into the efforts Rome had made towards leading these distant barbarians along the road to civilisation. The answer was – precious little: the planting of a colony of tough veterans on the site of the British capital and their chief religious centre, and a cornucopia of gifts and rewards to pro-Roman individuals. It was perhaps the stark contrast between the treatment towards the Trinovantes, all old and trusted allies of Rome, and the leaders of the community at Verulamium that must have aroused the most serious misgivings among those who may have been prepared to judge Rome by her actions. The seizure of the best lands for the 'model citizens' now turned out to be for an uncouth soldiery of the worse kind with a savage contempt for the British civilians. Then the building of the first Romanised city for the Britons at Verulamium, and the granting of municipal status, might have been seen by the rest of Britain as an act of sycophants fawning on their conquerors, while others who had actually helped Rome at the time of the conquest had suffered savage reprisals and bitter humiliation.

The people who had whole-heartedly embraced the cause of Rome were the inhabitants of what is now Kent, Sussex, Essex, Hertfordshire and Greater London. This was the extent, as we have seen, of the original Belgic settlement. Perhaps the Romans felt that this was their real foothold in Britain and their urban policy excluded the lands beyond this. But it was not enough. The string of military commanders sent to deal with the initial conquest, and with the subsequent hostility of the frontier tribes, had concentrated on their main task and had done little to advance the cause of Rome in the rearward areas. Ostorius Scapula had, in an ill-judged moment of panic, tried to terrorise the Britons into cowed submission to enable him to advance his troops to deal with Caratacus. This is the act which must have wiped away all the results of the smooth diplomacy and presented the Britons with the harsh political and military realities which underlay Roman policy towards her newly acquired peoples. The Druids exploited this turn of events, and, by playing on fears and deep religious beliefs, built up over the following decade, directed a wave of bitter hostility which almost engulfed the army, the administrators, the traders and those Britons who had overtly succumbed to the blandishments of Rome.

Conquests throughout the ages have presented this fascinating problem of the balance of power within the conquered community. No occupying force can ever operate effectively without some degree of local cooperation. Those who help the army always suffer opprobrium and are treated as traitors. Intense national pride, sometimes to the extreme of chauvinism, is a fairly modern phenomenon. In first-century Britain, such feelings were restricted to a sense of tribal unity and loyalty towards the reigning family. But underlying this were the deeper emotions aroused by Druidism, whose powerful priests used fear and superstition as their main agents against the enemy. The Romans clearly understood the sense of duty in its many aspects, since it was one of their own cherished tenets and, given time, could inculcate this relationship between the Britons and Rome, as of dependants towards their master; but it could only have come about in a period of peace and as new generations were born into the acceptance of Roman authority.

Religious fear and frenzy were regarded by the Romans of the old school as unnatural excesses. The old Roman virtues were based on moderation and sobriety, and religion was seen as a matter of obligation to the gods in performing time-honoured rituals at the proper times and in the proper places. When the exotic cults reached Rome from Egypt and the East, they were not readily accepted. Some were banned altogether and others only allowed in the outskirts of the town, much like the Nonconformist chapels in nineteenth-century England. Many of the educated Romans were Stoics, believers in a Greek philosophy which taught men to be self-sufficient and take a detached view of personal emotions. Its very austerity had an appeal – an obvious recent parallel is the traditional stiff upper lip of the upper-class Englishman. Modern religious rockers and rollers would have aroused the same feelings of distaste in these gentlemen as the frenzies of the worshippers of Isis did in the worthy citizens of Rome in the first century.

Yet there was an astonishing tolerance of other peoples' religions and this was largely due to the teaching of the older philosophies which abjured belief in the supernatural. The mass of the people firmly believed in the presence of unseen spirits everywhere, but each exercising a benign influence over a place, especially springs and rivers, provided they were acknowledged and placated. The only religions to which the Romans were totally opposed were those allied to political power, since the deep feeling they could generate could be turned against Roman authority. Perhaps it is not surprising that the most savage and devastating wars Rome ever fought were against the Jews and the Britons, since Judaism and Druidism had a strong political bias and the passions they aroused were directed against

Rome with a fanaticism which could be broken only by a crushing defeat that destroyed the majority of the devotees.

It is this which puts the Revolt into the same category as other religious wars. The same frenzies inspired the extraordinary advance of the followers of Mahomet, the terrible excesses in the Middle Ages, such as the reprisals against the Albigensians and those on St Bartholomew's Eve, both carried out under the name of Christianity, the basic tenets of which are peace and gentleness. The same religious turmoil is seen today in Ireland, and one cannot easily forget the Mau-Mau atrocities in Kenya in recent years. Today the religions which exercise such intensities of devotion among their followers are no longer based on supernatural powers, but are politically motivated. The forces once generated under the names of Christ and Mahomet are now more likely to be found under Marx, Lenin, Trotsky and Mao Tse-tung. They are all based ultimately on small groups of fanatics who seek to impose their will on large numbers of people, by the skilled use of envy and greed rather than through superstition, and by increasing tensions which always exist between racial groups and social classes. The small group always remains in the background preserving its anonymity, the operations are executed through puppets or front men, who are always expendable. Thus to the Druidic priesthood the troubles of Boudica were exploited to the full and she became the figurehead, drawing together all dissidents under her banner.

One could well ask if these tragic events have anything to teach us about our present difficulties, which seem at first to have little connection with such a remote piece of history. The answer surely is that human beings have changed very little. If we could understand more fully the factors behind the Revolt, and especially the attitude of the Roman government, we would be in a much better position to evaluate present politics. But there is too much we can never know and, only by making assessments of similar current events, can we see these distant happenings in their real perspective. This is a two-way process; for archaeologists and historians can offer their contributions to the understanding of our present troubles by showing how historical sequences at different times, and in different places, run in such close parallel.

The main lesson to be learnt is that one should try to penetrate beyond the surface appearance of events. Unfortunately, their presentation by the mass media has tended to be so oversimplified and to be so built around 'personalities', that it has become valueless as a basis of genuine assessment. There are so many levels of knowledge and one has to dig through them, like the archaeologist with his stratified deposits: only as one gets lower in the excavation is there full understanding. Even so, human problems can never be fully resolved unless attempts are made to understand what causes people to act as they do, accepting that in many cases they hardly know the reason themselves. A careful study of historical cause and effect helps us to appreciate the complexities of political issues of our own day. One of the lessons we might learn from the Revolt is that conquered people should be treated with sympathy and understanding, not with savagery and repression. Another could be that toleration has little chance of success against certain kinds of religious/political fanaticism, especially when small determined groups are working towards precise but narrow objectives, perhaps not discernible at the time. When toleration in a community degenerates into apathy, there is fertile ground for these small bodies of extremists to plant and nurture their seeds of disruption.

There are elements of all these things in the story of the events of AD 60, although much of it is misted over by lack of precise information. Those thoughtful for the future should study these and similar patterns of human behaviour. They may help us to see more clearly what is happening in the world today, and even help us prevent some of the worst excesses of human folly and greed for power, which brings incalculable misery and suffering to the innocent majority.

References

Abbreviations

BAR	British Archaeological Reports
BM	The British Museum
CBA	The Council for British Archaeology
CIL	*Corpus Inscriptionum Latinarum*
DOE	Department of the Environment
fn.	footnote
HMSO	Her Majesty's Stationery Office
OS	Ordnance Survey
RCHM	The Royal Commission on Historical Monuments
RIB	*Roman Inscriptions of Britain* i, 1965, Oxford
VCH	*Victoria County History*

The abbreviations used for periodicals conform to the standards established by the CBA.

Introduction

1 T. D. Kendrick, *British Antiquity*, 1949, pp. 79 f.

1 Sources

1 Duff, *Victoria in the Highlands*, 1968
2 I am most grateful to Professor Kenneth Jackson for his helpful comments.
3 *J. Roman Stud.*, (1921), pp. 101–7
4 *Année Epigraphique*, 1967, No 170 from Civitas Igaeditanorum. The text reads:

    L] ovio Caenonis f. patri
    Boudicae Tongi f. matri
    Cilio Tapaesi f. socro Cileae
    Cili f. uxori Caeno Lovi f.

(Caeno, son of Lovius [set this up] to his father, Lovius, son of Caeno and to his mother Boudica, daughter of Tongus and to his father-in-law, Cilius, son of Tapaesus, and to his wife, Cilea, daughter of Cilius.)

I am grateful to Dr John Mann for drawing my attention to this inscription

5 *Nero*, 39 and 18

6 Lewis Spence, *Boadicea, Warrior Queen of the Britons*, 1937, pp. 251–4

7 Excavation Section 1938, p. 5, published separately from the *Trans.*

8 *Excavation on Defence Sites*, 1934–45, i, 1960 (HMSO), the first of three volumes, the other two have yet to appear

9 *Rescue Archaeology*, ed. P. A. Rahtz, 1974

10 There are many studies of this fascinating subject from the pioneer studies by O. G. S. Crawford and A. Keiller, *Wessex from the Air*, 1928 and J. Bradford, *Ancient Landscapes*, 1957, to the recent technical review *Aerial Reconnaissance for Archaeology*, ed. by D. R. Wilson, CBA Research Report No. 12, 1975. The most important on the sites of Roman Britain has been by Professor J. K. St Joseph in a sequence of papers in the *J. Roman Stud.*, 1951, '53, '55, '58, '62, '65, '69 and '73

2   The Opposing Forces and the State of Britain 54 BC

1 There are useful introductory books such as: G. R. Watson, *The Roman Soldier*, 1969 (Thames and Hudson); Graham Webster, *The Roman Imperial Army*, 1969 (A. & C. Black) and Phil Barker, *The Armies and Enemies of Imperial Rome*, 1972 (War Games Publication)

2 See for example, David Breeze, 'Pay Grades and Ranks below the Centurionate', *J. Roman Stud.*, 61 (1971), pp. 133–5

3 H. Russell Robinson, *The Armour of Imperial Rome*, 1975 (Arms and Armour Press)

4 For a background to the Celts: T. G. E. Powell, *The Celts*, 1958; Anne Ross, *Pagan Celtic Britain*, 1967 (Routledge); and *Everyday Life of the Pagan Celts*, 1970 (Batsford)

5 Sir Cyril Fox, *Antiq. J.*, 27 (1947), p. 117

6 See the Introduction to the OS *Map of Southern Britain in the Iron Age*, 1962, pp. 19–32. The dates of the Gallo–Belgic coins given here and in the text above have been challenged by Simone Sheers (*Brit. Numismatic J.*' 41 (1972), 1–6). If this view is accepted, some revisions will be necessary

7 'Coinage, Oppida and the Rise of Belgic Power in South-Eastern Britain' in *Oppida in Barbarian Europe*, 1976 (BAR), pp. 181–312

8 'The Aylesford Swarling Culture: The Problems of the Belgae Reconsidered', *Proc. Prehist. Soc.*, 31 (1965), pp. 241–367

9 See map on fig. 71 in D. W. Harding's, *The Iron Age in Lowland Britain*, 1974 (Routledge)

10 See note 7 above, fig. 7

11 See note 8 above

12 *Archaeologia*, 52 (1890), pp. 317–88

13 J. Boardman, *The Greeks Overseas*, 1973 ed., p. 210

14 'Roman Amphorae in Pre-Roman Britain', *The Iron Age and its Hill Forts*, ed. by M. Jesson and D. Hill, 1971, pp. 161–88

15 J. P. Bushe-Fox, *Excavations at Hengistbury Head, Hampshire in 1911–12*, 1915, Soc. of Antiquaries Research Report No. 3

3   Britain between the Invasions 54 BC–AD 43

1 See Chapter 2, note 14 above
2 This has been taken with his permission from his fig. 36 with additions by Warwick Rodwell (fn. 7, chap. 2)
3 For the importance of Hengistbury Head as a port of entry and for trade see B. Cunliffe, 'The Hillforts and Oppida in Britain', *Problems in Economic and Social Archaeology*, ed. G. de G. Sieveking, I. A. Longworth and K. E. Wilson, 1976, pp. 343–58
4 *Britannia*, 1967, p. 41
5 OS *Map of the Iron Age in Southern Britain*, map 4; also Warwick Rodwell, fig. 28
6 'Britain between the Invasions (BC 54 – AD 43): A Study in Ancient Diplomacy', *Aspects of Archaeology in Britain and Beyond*, ed. W. F. Grimes, 1951, pp. 332–44
7 *Geography* ii, 5, 8; iv, 5, 5
8 *Britannia*, 1967, p. 44
9 A suggestion put to me by Geoff Dannell
10 'Cunobelin's Gold', *Britannia*, 6 (1975), pp 1-19
11 For the background see C. M. Wells, *The German Policy of Augustus*, (Oxford), 1972
12 See fn. 4
13 See fn. 7, chap. 2, fig. 51
14 C. F. C. Hawkes and M. R. Hull, *Camulodunum*, 1947, Soc. of Antiquaries Research Report, No. 14
15 R. P. Mack, *The Coinage of Ancient Britain*, 1952 (Spink), pp. 127, 130–2
16 E. A. Sydenham, *The Roman Republican Coinage*, 1952
17 I. M. Stead, *The La Tène Cultures of East Yorkshire*, 1965
18 R. R. Clarke, 'The Early Iron Age Treasure from Snettisham, Norfolk', *Proc. Prehist. Soc.*, 20 (1954), pp. 27–86
19 J. W. Brailsford, 'The Sedgeford Torc', *Prehistoric and Roman Studies*, 1971 (BM), pp. 16–19 and pls. VI and VII
20 ibid, pls. CIII and IX
21 R. Rainbird Clarke, 'The Iron Age in Norfolk and Suffolk', *Archaeol. J.*, 96 (1939), pp. 82–90
22 'The Coins of the Iceni', *Britannia*, 1 (1970), pp. 1–33
23 See R. Rainbird Clarke, *East Anglia*, 1960, fig. 26
24 A suggestion made by R. Rainbird Clarke, *British Numismatic J.*, 28 (1956), p. 51, and accepted by Derek Allen
25 *Britannia*, 7 (1976), pp. 276–8; 10 (1979), pp. 258–9
26 See Dr Peacock's distribution map, fig. 38
27 See the contributions of Valery Rigby and Kevin Greene in *Current Research in Romano-British Coarse Pottery*, CBA, Research Report No. 10, 1973
28 I. M. Stead, 'A La Tène III Burial at Welwyn Garden City', *Archaeologia*, 101 (1967), pp. 1–62; the cups are also illustrated in D. W. Harding's, *The Iron Age in Lowland Britain*, 1974, pl. XXVII
29 R. A. Smith, 'On Late-Celtic Antiquities discovered at Welwyn, Herts', *Archaeologia*, 63, (1912), pp. 1–30

I

30 P. G. Laver, 'The Excavations of a Tumulus at Lexden, Colchester', *Archaeo-logia*, 76 (1927), pp. 241–54; see also I. Stead, 'The Earliest burials of the Aylesford culture', *Problems in Economic and Social Archaeology*, ed. G. de G. Sieveking, I. A. Longworth and K. E. Wilson, 1976, pp. 401–6

31 *A Guide to the Exhibition illustrating Greek and Roman Life*, (BM), 1929, fig. 101

32 This is illustrated with another on a seated figure now at Aix-en-Provence and the Roman auxiliary equivalents by Russell Robinson, see fn. 1, pls. 461 and 468, etc

33 *Caligula*, 44, 2

34 'Did Adminius strike coins?', *Britannia*, 7 (1976), pp. 96–100

35 This has been carefully studied by Professor C. F. C. Hawkes in E. M. Clifford, *Bagendon, a Belgic Oppidum*, 1961, pp. 1961, pp. 60–2

36 *Iron Age Communities in Britain*, 1974, p. 71

37 Professor S. S. Frere, *Britannia*, p. 50

38 'The samian from Bagendon', *Roman Pottery Studies in Britain and Beyond*, ed. J. Dore and K. Greene, (BAR), 1977,229–34

39 Dio, lx, 19

4 The Conquest of AD 43

1 For a fuller account see G. Webster and D. R. Dudley, *The Roman Conquest of Britain* (Pan paperback), 1973

2 *RIB*, No. 61

3 *CIL*, vi, 920

4 i.e. the rulers of the Regni, Atrebates, Iceni, Dobunni, Coritani, Trinovantes, Brigantes

5 *Annals* VII to X of Tacitus, covering the period AD 38–46, are missing, but the story of Britain starts again with the arrival of Scapula (XII, 31)

6 *Annals*, 3, 42

7 The best recent account is Stuart Piggott, *The Druids* (Penguin), 1974

8 ibid. p. 37 and T. G. E. Powell, *The Celts*, 1958, pl. 76 and pp. 274–5

9 Anne Ross, *Pagan Celtic Britain*, 1967, pp. 61–126

10 *Prehistoric and Roman Studies*, ed. by G. de G. Sieveking (BM), 1971, pl. XC and fig. 4 on p. 263

11 A full account of this work has not yet been published, but there are brief accounts in *Archaeology*, 1 (1948), 74–8, and *Problems of the Iron Age in Southern Britain*, ed. S. S. Frere, 25–8

12 *A Find of the Early Iron Age from Llyn Cerrig Bach, Anglesey*, National Museum of Wales, 1946; see also F. Lynch, *Prehistoric Anglesey*, 1970, pp. 249-77

13 A. E. Gordon 'Quintus Veranius, Consul AD 49', *University of California, Papers on Classical Archaeol.*, 2, pp. 231–75, 1952

5 The Storm Breaks AD 60

1 Josephus, *Wars of the Jews*, II, i–vi

2 'Templum Divo Claudio Constitutum', *Britannia*, 3 (1972), 164–81

3 Tiberius rode 200 miles in 24 hours to be at the bedside of his dying brother Drusus in Germany, while Julius Caesar reckoned to do 100 miles a day by coach
4 George C. Boon, *Silchester: The Roman Town of Calleva*, 1974, p. 46
5 *Agricola*, 14
6 A. Birley 'Agricola, the Flavian Dynasty, and Tacitus' in *The Ancient Historian and his Materials*, ed. by Barbara Levick, 1975, pp. 139–54
7 Suetonius, *Titus*, 4

6 The Evidence from the Ground

1 OS, 1962, see chap. 2, fn 6, p. 136
2 *Proc. Prehistoric Soc.*, 17 (1951), pp. 214–25
3 As demonstrated by Morna Macgregor, *Early Celtic Art in North Britain*, (Leicester), 1976, Map 7, p. 65; see also C.N. Moore, *Brit.*, 4 (1973) pp. 153 ff.
4 36, (1855), pl. XXXVII and pp. 454–6
5 fn. 3 above, fig. 1
6 R. A. Smith, *Proc. Cambridge Antiq. Soc.*, 13 for 1908–9, pp. 146–63; also *V.C.H. Suffolk*, i, 1911, pp. 321–3
7 *Britannia*, 6 (1975), p. 206
8 J. M. C. Toynbee and R. R. Clark, 'A decorated helmet and other objects from Norfolk', *J. Roman Stud.*, 38 (1948), pp. 20–7
9 fn. 3, chap. 2, pls. 384–6, p. 131
10 *Proc. Suffolk Inst. of Archaeol.*, 23 (1939), pp. 173–4
11 *The Archaeology of the Cambridge Region*, 1923
12 *East Anglia*, 1960, p. 114
13 *J. Roman Stud.*, 35 (1945), p. 82
14 *Antiq. J.*, 36 (1956), pp. 73–5
15 A coloured illustration appears in *Roman Crafts*, 1976, pl. II
16 *Art in Britain under the Romans*, 1964, p. 49 and pl. V
17 95, pp. 291–3
18 In the *Trans. Birmingham and Warks. Archaeol. Soc.*, 1969, 1971 and 1975
19 ibid, 79 (1964), pp. 117–20
20 ibid, 85 (1973), pp. 211–3 and pl. 35
21 *Current Arch.*, 125 (1991), pp.210–14

7 The Trail of Destruction

1 H. Hurst, 'Excavations at Gloucester, 1968–71: First Interim Report' *Antiq. J.*, 52 (1972), pp. 24–69
2 M. R. Hull, *Roman Colchester*, 1958, Soc. of Antiquaries Research Report No. 20
3 Philip Crummy, *Colchester, Recent Excavations and Research*, 1974 (Colchester Excavation Committee)
4 B. R. K. Dunnett, 'Excavations 1964–8', *Trans. Essex Archaeol. Soc.*, 3, 3rd ser. (1971), p. 12
5 fn. 2, p. 104
6 *J. Roman Stud.*, 9 (1919), pp. 139–69; 10 (1920), pp. 87–9

7 *Trans. Essex Archaeol. Soc.* 25 (1955), pp. 24–61

8 fn. 4, pp. 115–30

9 fn. 4, pp. 98–129

10 fn. 2, p. 86

11 May, *Catalogue of Roman Pottery in the Castle Museum*, 1930, pl. XXXI, No. 133

12 *Archaeol. J.*, 101 (1946), pp. 68–90

13 *RIB*, No. 201

14 The letters on the stone are ī VA[. . . followed by a letter which begins with an upright, thus, the name of the unit could have been VANGIONVM or VARDVLLORVM, and the former is preferred

15 The group is well illustrated in J. M. C. Toynbee, *Art in Britain under the Romans* (OUP), 1964, pl. XCVI

16 RCHM, *Roman London*, 1928, p. 15

17 'Two Fires of Roman London', *Antiq. J.*, 25 (1945), pp. 48–77

18 R. Merrifield, *The Roman City of London*, 1965, p. 37 and fig. 3

19 Peter Marsden, 'The Excavations of a Roman Palace Site in London, 1961–72', *Trans. London and Middlesex Archaeol. Soc.*, 26 (1975), pp. 1–102

20 'Excavations at Aldgate and Bush Lane House in the City of London, 1972', *Trans. London and Middlesex Archaeol. Soc.*, 24 (1973), pp. 4–7

21 R. E. M. and T. V. Wheeler, *Verulamium, A Belgic and two Roman Cities*, 1936, Soc. of Antiquaries Research Report No. 11

22 *Antiq. J.*, 36 (1956), pp. 7–10

23 *Verulamium Excavations* I, Soc. of Antiquaries Research Report No. 28

24 *Archaeological Excavations 1975*, DOE (HMSO), p. 61

25 *Proc.* 2nd ser. XXII, No. 11, pp. 343–4; *J. Roman Stud.*, 16 (1926), pp. 3–6

26 See fn. 15, pp. 46–8

27 *Classical Review*, March 1974

28 fn. 15, pp. 302–3 and pl. LXX

29 *Proc. Suffolk Inst. of Archaeol.* 31 (1970), pp. 57–63

30 M. Grant, *Gladiators*, Pelican ed. 1971, pp. 45–7

31 *Annals* iii, 43

32 *RIB*, No. 9

33 *Illustrations of Roman London*, RCHM, *Roman London*, 1928, pl. 22

34 *Antiq. J.*, 16 (1936), pp. 1–7

35 *RIB*, No. 108

36 E. M. Wightman, *Roman Trier* (Hart-Davis), 1970, p. 39

Short Bibliography

Classical sources

Caesar, *de Bello Gallico*
Dio Cassius, *Historia Romana*, LXII
Suetonius, *de vita Caesarum*
Tacitus, *Agricola*
Tacitus, *Annals*, XIV

Modern works

Barry Cunliffe, *Iron Age Communities in Britain* (Routledge), 1974
Barry Cunliffe and Trevor Rowley ed., *Oppida in Barbarian Europe* (BAR), 1976
D. W. Harding, *The Iron Age in Lowland Britain* (Routledge), 1974
S. S. Frere, *Britannia*, 3rd ed. 1978
Stuart Piggott, *The Druids*, (Pelican), 1974
Anne Ross, *Pagan Celtic Britain* (Routledge), 1967
Anne Ross, *Everyday Life of the Pagan Celts* (Batsford), 1970
John Wacher, *The Coming of Rome* (Routledge), 1979
Graham Webster and Donald Dudley, *The Roman Conquest of Britain* (Pan), 1973
Graham Webster, *The British Celts and their Gods under Rome* (Batsford), 1986
Graham Webster, *The Roman Imperial Army* (Black), 1969
Ordnance Survey, *Map of Roman Britain*, 1978
Ordnance Survey, *Map of Southern Britain in the Iron Age*, 1962

Glossary of Latin Terms and Words (plural ending in brackets)

ala(-e)   An auxiliary cavalry unit of 500 or 1000

amphora(-e)   A large container for transporting wine and oil

auxilia   A general term for the units secondary to, but supporting the legions

beneficiarius(-i)   Normally an old soldier seconded for civilian duties such as customs and tax officers, or for police work

civitas(-ates)   A term given to a tribal area including its capital

clades Variana   The disaster of Varus

cohors (cohortes)   An auxiliary unit of wholly or part-mounted infantry of 500 or 1000

cohors(-tes) equitata(-e)   A part-mounted infantry unit

colonia(-e)   A settlement of retired army veterans, also the title given to existing cities, giving them municipal status

curia(-e)   The building in which the City 'Council' (*ordo*) held its meetings

decurio(-nes)   An officer in command of the *turma* (squadron) of an *ala*, also a town councillor

denarius(-i)   A small Roman silver coin, 25 of which equalled the gold *aureus*

duplicarius(-i)   An auxiliary officer, so named because his pay was double that of the men

gemina(-e)   (literally a twin) – a term given to the two legions created by splitting a single one, as with *Legio XIV Gemina*

gyrus   An arena for training horses

insula(-e)   A term for a block in the street grid plan of a city

legatus legionis   A legionary commander

legio(-nes)   A legion of heavy armoured foot soldiers

libertus(-i)   A freedman

lorica(-e) hamata(-e)   A cuirass made of mail

lorica(-e) segmenta(-e)   A cuirass made of horizontal strips of steel, held together internally by leather strips, giving freedom of movement, as worn by legionaries

lorica(-e) squamata(-e)   A cuirass made of overlapping scales

milliary   of a unit of 1000 strong

mortarium(-a)   A kitchen vessel used for pulverising food

municipium(-a)   A town with a charter, giving it independent status, as also with a *colonia*

Oceanus   The god of the Oceans

oppidum(-a)   A fortified native settlement or stronghold

pagus(-i)   A country district

pax Romana   The Roman peace

praefectus castrorum   The camp prefect of a legion, an administrative office held by an equestrian, and who was third in the chain of command below the *legatus* and senior *tribunus*

primus pilus (primipilares)   The chief centurion of a legion who commanded the 1st cohort. The rank gives him equestrian status after a year's service.

quaestor(-es)   A junior magistrate in a town with financial responsibilities

quingenarius   of a unit of 500

quinquennales   Men appointed from a town council (*ordo*) every five years to organise the appropriate religious ceremonies

Res Gestae   The name given to the acts of Augustus which he considered worthy of record

rex   King, equivalent to the Celtic *ricomus*

severi augustales   Men appointed in a province to take part in the ceremonies of the Imperial cult.

sesterce(-s)   A small silver coin of the early Empire, equivalent to $2\frac{1}{2}$ *asses* (16 *asses* = 1 *denarius*)

toga(-e)   The garment signifying Roman citizenship and worn on official occasions

tribunus(-i) laticlavius(-i)   The senior tribune of a legion who had to be a senator designate, the other five *tribuni* were all of the equestrian order

vexillatio   a group of mixed units formed as an independent corps

victrix   victorious – a title given to a legion as *Legio* XX *Valeria Victrix*

vituus   a vine stick, the symbol of office of a legionary centurion

Index